THE LEARNING HEA

MW00650539

PROCURING INTEROPERABILITY

ACHIEVING HIGH-QUALITY, CONNECTED,
AND PERSON-CENTERED CARE

Peter Pronovost, Michael M. E. Johns, Sezin Palmer,
Raquel C. Bono, Douglas B. Fridsma, Andrew Gettinger,
Julian Goldman, William Johnson, Meredith Karney,
Craig Samitt, Ram D. Sriram, Ashwini Zenooz,
and Y. Claire Wang, *Editors*

NATIONAL ACADEMY OF MEDICINE

WASHINGTON, DC
NAM.EDU

NATIONAL ACADEMY OF MEDICINE • 500 FIFTH STREET, NW • WASHINGTON, DC 20001

Support for this publication was provided by the Gordon and Betty Moore Foundation, which fosters path-breaking scientific discovery, environmental conservation, patient care improvements and preservation of the special character of the Bay Area.

Library of Congress Cataloging-in-Publication Data

Names: Pronovost, Peter J., editor. | National Academy of Medicine (U.S.), issuing body.
Title: Procuring interoperability : achieving high-quality, connected, and person-centered care / Peter Pronovost [and 12 others], editors.
Description: Washington, DC : NAM.EDU, [2018] | Series: Learning health system series | Includes bibliographical references.
Identifiers: LCCN 2018041809 (print) | LCCN 2018042655 (ebook) | ISBN 9781947103139 (E-book) | ISBN 9781947103122 (pbk. : alk. paper)
Subjects: | MESH: Medical Informatics Applications | Purchasing, Hospital | Systems Integration | Software
Classification: LCC R855.3 (ebook) | LCC R855.3 (print) | NLM WX 26.5 | DDC 610.285--dc23
LC record available at https://lccn.loc.gov/2018041809

Suggested citation: Pronovost, P., M. M. E. Johns, S. Palmer, R. C. Bono, D. B. Fridsma, A. Gettinger, J. Goldman, W. Johnson, M. Karney, C. Samitt, R. D. Sriram, A. Zenooz, and Y. C. Wang, Editors. 2018. *Procuring Interoperability: Achieving High-Quality, Connected, and Person-Centered Care.* Washington, DC: National Academy of Medicine.

"Knowing is not enough; we must apply.
Willing is not enough; we must do."

—GOETHE

LEADERSHIP

IMPACT

for a healthier future

NATIONAL ACADEMY OF MEDICINE

ABOUT THE NATIONAL ACADEMY OF MEDICINE

The **National Academy of Medicine** is one of three Academies constituting the National Academies of Sciences, Engineering, and Medicine (the National Academies). The National Academies provide independent, objective analysis and advice to the nation and conduct other activities to solve complex problems and inform public policy decisions. The National Academies also encourage education and research, recognize outstanding contributions to knowledge, and increase public understanding in matters of science, engineering, and medicine.

The **National Academy of Sciences** was established in 1863 by an Act of Congress, signed by President Lincoln, as a private, nongovernmental institution to advise the nation on issues related to science and technology. Members are elected by their peers for outstanding contributions to research. Dr. Marcia McNutt is president.

The **National Academy of Engineering** was established in 1964 under the charter of the National Academy of Sciences to bring the practices of engineering to advising the nation. Members are elected by their peers for extraordinary contributions to engineering. Dr. C. D. Mote, Jr. is president.

The **National Academy of Medicine** (formerly the Institute of Medicine) was established in 1970 under the charter of the National Academy of Sciences to advise the nation on issues of health, health care, and biomedical science and technology. Members are elected by their peers for distinguished contributions to medicine and health. Dr. Victor J. Dzau is president.

Learn more about the National Academy of Medicine at NAM.edu.

STEERING COMMITTEE

PETER PRONOVOST, Johns Hopkins Medicine (Chair)
MICHAEL M. E. JOHNS, Emory University (Co-Chair)
SEZIN PALMER, Johns Hopkins Applied Physics Lab (Co-Chair)
RAQUEL C. BONO, US Department of Defense
DOUGLAS B. FRIDSMA, American Medical Informatics Association
ANDREW GETTINGER, Office of the National Coordinator of Health IT
JULIAN GOLDMAN, Massachusetts General Hospital
WILLIAM JOHNSON, WMJ Associates, LLC
MEREDITH KARNEY, Center for Medical Interoperability
CRAIG SAMITT, Anthem, Inc.
RAM D. SRIRAM, National Institute of Standards and Technology
ASHWINI ZENOOZ, US Department of Veterans Affairs

NAM Staff

Development of this publication was facilitated by contributions of the following NAM staff, under the guidance of J. Michael McGinnis, Leonard D. Schaeffer Executive Officer and Executive Director of the Leadership Consortium for a Value & Science-Driven Health System:

Y. CLAIRE WANG, Project Director (from July 2017)
MARIANNE HAMILTON LOPEZ, Project Director (until July 2017)
MAHNOOR AHMED, Research Associate
JESSICA BROWN, Executive Assistant to the Executive Officer
VANANH VO, Senior Program Assistant (until July 2017)
ROSHEEN BIRDIE, Senior Program Assistant (until September 2016)
UROOJ FATIMA, Senior Program Assistant (until March 2018)
LAURA DeSTEFANO, Director of Communications
MOLLY DOYLE, Communications Specialist (until April 2018)
JENNA L. OGILVIE, Communications Officer

Consultant

EMILY PAULSEN, rapporteur

REVIEWERS

This special publication was reviewed in draft form by individuals chosen for their diverse perspectives and technical expertise, in accordance with review procedures established by the National Academy of Medicine. We wish to thank the following individuals for their contributions:

JULIA ADLER-MILSTEIN, University of California, San Francisco
JOHN BERNOT, National Quality Forum
KAREN DESALVO, Dell Medical School, The University of Texas at Austin
MARK E. FRISSE, Vanderbilt University Medical Center
JIM N. JIRJIS, Hospital Corporation of America
THOMAS M. LEARY, HIMSS North America
JONATHAN B. PERLIN, Hospital Corporation of America
MATTHEW QUINN, Health Resources and Services Administration
GENEVIEVE MORRIS, Office of the National Coordinator for Health IT
WENDY NILSEN, National Science Foundation
WILLIAM W. STEAD, Vanderbilt University Medical Center
VINDELL WASHINGTON, Blue Cross and Blue Shield of Louisiana
SANDY WEININGER, US Food and Drug Administration

The reviewers listed above provided many constructive comments and suggestions, but they were not asked to endorse the content of the publication, and did not see the final draft before it was published. Review of this publication was overseen by **Y. Claire Wang,** Senior Program Advisor, NAM; and **J. Michael McGinnis,** Leonard D. Schaeffer Executive Officer, NAM. Responsibility for the final content of this publication rests entirely with the editors and the NAM.

ACKNOWLEDGMENTS

We would like to thank Drs. Jennifer Lee and Brook Watts, formerly with the US Department of Veterans Affairs, for contributing to earlier drafts of this publication, as well as Dr. Marianne Hamilton Lopez for her service as Project Director through July 2017.

We would also like to thank Daniel Bearss with the National Academies of Sciences, Engineering, and Medicine for contributing to the development of this publication through fact-checking assistance.

CONTENTS

FOREWORD

The National Academy of Medicine (NAM) and the Gordon and Betty Moore Foundation are pleased to partner in the development and release of *Procuring Interoperability: Achieving High-Quality, Connected, and Person-Centered Care*. As medical knowledge, diagnostic tools, and treatment options grow at an unparalleled pace, and as digital technology offers a platform to transform delivery of care, the potential for improving health and health care is enormous. At the same time, an equally vast gap separates what we know should be possible through digital technology and the results we actually achieve.

Economic incentives have driven the evolution of a health system that is fragmented, inefficient, and ineffective in matching identified needs with available resources. The result is health care expenditures that are highest in the world coupled with system-wide performance that ranks far below most other countries with similar economic profiles.

In no arena is fragmentation more blatantly exposed than in the pervasive lack of interoperability in the digital health and health care infrastructure. Connected care is the goal; disconnected care is the reality. Despite the fact that the use of certified electronic health records grew in less than two decades from nearly non-existent to 2016 levels of more than 95 percent in hospitals and 75 percent in ambulatory care settings, actual interoperability is very limited for most digital tools, including health records, devices, and mobile applications.

Multiple devices used in the care of a single patient often operate on different platforms. Even in a single organization, different units often cannot seamlessly access needed health information and virtually absent are functional digital exchange capacities among different organizations and systems. Efficiency is defeated when too many records can be shared only in hard copy form, too many monitors operate independently, too many clinicians spend too much time processing and rectifying paperwork, and too many patients and families cannot access the information they need.

Clinicians are thus hampered in the delivery of the coordinated care both they and patients desire, and they are frustrated. Uncoordinated care and the delays, misdirections, and omissions it produces, lead to avoidable harm to patients.

The 1999 Institute of Medicine (now National Academy of Medicine) publication, *To Err is Human: Building a Safer Health System,* alerted the nation to striking safety and quality shortfalls in health care, prompting important, life-saving initiatives through better infection control, surgical protocols, medication management, and health care environmental engineering. Today, the increasing complexity in health care, the need for more seamless interfaces among clinicians, patients and families, and the increasing urgency of linking health care with social service interventions for high-need patients, has made digital interoperability even more essential across clinicians, care units, facilities, and systems. The absence of digital interoperability is no longer acceptable.

Although interoperability has been a topic of national health policy discussions for more than a decade, the pace of progress has been handicapped by limited agreement on requisite standards, divergent incentives and agendas among vendors, and notably, by disparate and inconsistent characteristics in user purchasing strategies, practices, and emphases. When it comes to procuring digital services for health and health care systems, interoperability is simply not yet an effectively structured component of either the supply or the demand equations, nor of the links between the two.

This publication, *Procuring Interoperability: Achieving High-Quality, Connected, and Person-Centered Care,* provides a summary of a project commissioned by the Gordon and Betty Moore Foundation to explore procurement approaches health care systems can use to activate system-wide demand for interoperability in health care, and to work together for its accomplishment. Experts representing various core health and health care stakeholders—clinicians, health systems, health insurers, informatics, standards organizations, government health systems—were engaged by the NAM to undertake that exploration through consultations, public meetings, literature reviews, and frequent conference calls. An important element of the consultations was a January 2018 NAM convening of more than 70 leaders from the stakeholder communities to review a preliminary summary of the findings and to offer insights on the most prominent issues and priorities moving forward. Drawing on those conversations, supplemented by comments solicited from a number of additional experts and reviewers, this NAM Special Publication has been developed as a summary of the issues and approaches. Most importantly, it presents elements of a roadmap for moving forward.

We would like to convey the gratitude of both the NAM and the Gordon and Betty Moore Foundation to each of the editors and contributors to this work, in particular to steering group co-chairs Peter Pronovost, Michael Johns, and Sezin Palmer. We would also like to acknowledge the project directors Drs.

Marianne Lopez Hamilton and Claire Wang for their leadership in shepherding the development that so nicely sets the stage for follow-on progress.

The potential for progress is extraordinary. Our emerging digital world offers the prospect of revolutionary transformation in the pace and accuracy with which problems are identified, and in the precision with which solutions are targeted. The technology exists, and is improving daily, to build the needed, seamless digital platform. Now is the time for clinical providers and other purchasers to ensure that each digital tool purchased for use in health and health care can seamlessly interface and cooperate on behalf of people everywhere. If each health care leader works to realize that aim, they will greatly benefit the health of everyone.

J. Michael McGinnis, MD, MPP
Leonard Schaeffer Executive Officer
National Academy of Medicine

Harvey V. Fineberg, MD, PhD
President
Gordon and Betty Moore Foundation

PREFACE

Our health care delivery system requires unprecedented access to health information in order to effectively and efficiently provide the best care to individual patients and entire populations. Access to relevant and useful data that allows clinicians to meet the demands of modern health care becomes essential for building a continuously learning health system that supports new models of care, outcomes-based reimbursement, and personalized medicine. Such achievement will depend on the degree of interoperability among all the component systems of the health care system and medical devices. While health care has made great strides in recent years with the proliferation of electronic health records, the establishment of regional health information exchanges, and the development of data exchange standards and interfaces, true interoperability remains an elusive goal. True interoperability is the ability to seamlessly and automatically deliver data when and where it is needed under a trusted network without political, technical, or financial blocking.

Leading health care organizations are beginning to recognize that future sustainability and competitive advantage will be driven by their ability to deliver safe, efficient, and economical care—and comprehensive data interoperability is absolutely crucial to this transformation. In contrast to many other industries, the purchasers of health care technology have not fully leveraged their individual or collective purchasing power to require interoperability from the health technology marketplace. With better procurement practices, supported by the establishment of shared interoperability platform and architecture, health care systems can prepare themselves to advance much more rapidly into the person-centric health care environment of the future.

This National Academy of Medicine (NAM) special publication convenes a multistakeholder group of experts to examine the state of health care technology purchasing and to chart a path toward achieving large-scale interoperability through strategic acquisition of health technology, medical devices, and software applications. Over the course of eighteen months, the steering committee and NAM staff developed the goals, framework, and change agents that will be required in the journey to realize an interoperable health system. With the assistance of the Johns Hopkins University Applied Physics Laboratory, the Center for Medical Interoperability, the Office of the National Coordinator for Health IT, and other industry consortia, this assessment reviews requirements for interoperable data exchange at three levels: facility-to-facility (macro-tier), intra-facility (meso-tier), and at point-of-care (micro-tier).

This publication outlines a tangible process to progress from the current state of health care systems with limited interoperability to the envisioned future state of health care systems with fully interoperable systems. Through the diverse perspectives brought to the discussion, we identified a multistep process , along with supporting details in the Technical Supplement, to assist health care organizations in establishing a process to ensure interoperability. The recognition that leading health care organizations will be best served by agreeing to a common approach that can be more broadly shared across institutions is also highlighted. The analytic framework employed considers key characteristics of information exchange involved in the three tiers of interoperability and focuses on the nature of the requirements for functional interoperability in care processes, the mapping of those requirements onto prevailing contracting practices, the specification of the steps necessary to achieve system-wide interoperability, and the proposal of a roadmap to use procurement specifications to engage those steps.

On January 30, 2018, the NAM convened a one-day meeting and discussion involving nearly 70 health care delivery system leaders and related stakeholders with the goal of eliciting perspectives and experience from the field. The valuable feedback from this meeting provided critical insight that was incorporated into the final version of this publication. Meeting participants stressed the need to support consumer- and patient-centered care delivery in a cost-effective and equitable manner and highlighted the fact that health technology procurement power is only one of many factors at play. Regulations, incentives, and other market forces must align and converge to truly move the needle.

In moving ahead, the fundamental responsibility lies within the cooperation among health care system leaders, as they guide progress within their own institutions, establish the organizational priority, marshal the expertise, and shape relevant acquisition strategies and interoperability requirements for purchases of digital technology. This cooperation requires solid and active commitment to collaboration that yields a multi-institutional strategy to develop and align on common contracting requirements to move toward the next generation of interoperable health systems.

Health care delivery and its technology infrastructure are approaching a critical juncture. Standards development and electronic health records adoption over the past decades have laid a fertile ground for an era of data liquidity where key information flows across the care continuum—and across the life cycle—helping clinicians to make better decisions at the right time for the right person. In the marketplace, it is also a critical time to ensure that competition among health care providers and technology vendors is focused on quality and value, rather than on exclusivity and proprietorship of data.

Strategic procurement holds exciting potential to move the health system toward true interoperability, especially when combined with the right policy and market incentives. It takes strong leadership and negotiation from many stakeholders, including health care providers, health technology vendors, societies and associations, standards organizations, federal agencies, and payers. Most importantly, clinicians and patients must be part of the process in order to improve patient safety, reduce burden, and enable learning and transformational care delivery models. The learning health care system that we envision is not possible without interoperability, and we have an obligation to improve health care so that future generations will have better lives. The time is now to realize the true potential of health information technology.

Peter Pronovost   Michael M. E. Johns   Sezin Palmer
Johns Hopkins University   Emory University   Johns Hopkins University

EXECUTIVE SUMMARY

The rapid movement of digital technology into all aspects of health and health care sets the stage for truly transformational opportunities to improve effectiveness, efficiency, and safety in health care as well as to envision the achievement of a health system that continuously learns and improves. However, that achievement will depend on the degree of system interoperability: the ability to share information across time and space from multiple devices, sources, and organizations. Although standards development and research on achieving safe interoperable systems have contributed to enhanced health information technology (IT) interoperability, much more work is needed (JASON, 2013; Rahurkar, Vest et al., 2015; Holmgren, Patel et al., 2017).

In other industries that have achieved a high degree of IT interoperability, standards support the work, yet its achievement is also simultaneously driven by vendor action and the demand from purchasers and users of technology. In health care, leveraging procurement specifications remains an important yet underused approach to drive health care integration, quality improvement, and cost containment. With better procurement practices that facilitate the acquisition of a fully interoperable digital infrastructure—electronic health record (EHR) systems, medical devices, and remote-site reporting tools—health care systems will advance much more rapidly into the health care environment of the future.

In this paper, we explore the state of play in the development and acquisition of interoperable health IT solutions and devices. Although we recognize that there are various ways to describe and categorize interoperability, in this paper we consider data exchanges in three levels: facility-to-facility (macro-tier), intra-facility (meso-tier), and at the point of care (micro-tier). To support health care transformation toward value-driven, whole-person care, interoperability is required across and among all three levels. The Technical Supplement further describes the necessary elements for each health care organization: an organization-wide interoperability steering group, a long-range interoperability road map, an interoperability needs identification process, and an interoperability procurement specification process.

To counter the prevailing challenges for acquiring interoperable technologies in a sustainable and cost-effective fashion, we propose an acquisition strategy applicable to health systems with different needs and serving diverse patients. Progress is particularly needed at the point-of-care level, where the lack of plug-and-play interoperability represents a fundamental impediment to patient safety, care coordination, and cost reduction. Rather than placing a narrow focus on price and features in the procurement of *each product*, health systems should establish a comprehensive, ongoing procurement strategy demanding functional *system-wide* interoperability. The goal is for health care systems to move away from serial purchases of individual software and hardware with proprietary interfaces, toward purchasing certified technologies that will interoperate with others through a vendor-neutral open platform.

We have identified five action priorities for each health care organization and system leader:

1. **Commit.** Declare interoperability a primary priority and form an organization-wide interoperability steering group or related capacity to champion the IT acquisition strategy.
2. **Identify.** Charge this group with identifying the set of interoperability goals, requirements, and model use cases for the procurement process to support organizational priorities and patient outcome goals.
3. **Collaborate.** Create a sector-wide strategy and partner with other stakeholders to align on common contracting requirements and specifications to move toward the next generation of interoperable health IT.
4. **Specify.** Use the collaboratively developed specifications to state clear functional interoperability requirements in existing and future proposals, purchases, and contracts.
5. **Assess.** Establish and monitor short-term and long-term metrics for the progress and contributions of interoperability to system-wide learning and improvement of health outcomes.

Standards-based, industry-driven, and modular acquisition of truly interoperable products is necessary for health care delivery systems to achieve the desired care quality, safety, and efficiency. It is important for health systems to work collaboratively in developing shared technical requirements for procuring industry solutions, as well as in moving toward an agreed-upon open architecture layer for seamless end-to-end interoperability and data exchange in the long run.

The interoperable infrastructure envisioned is also necessary for patients and families to be full partners, decision makers, and managers of their care. Only then will the health care industry begin to create truly integrated care systems that continuously provide better experiences for clinicians and patients while achieving better health and health care at lower cost.

I.

WHY INTEROPERABILITY IS ESSENTIAL IN HEALTH CARE

Spurred by several policy initiatives, most notably the Health Information Technology for Economic and Clinical Health (HITECH) Act of 2009, health care in the United States has experienced a steeply upward adoption curve of electronic health records (EHR) technology. As of 2016, 96 percent of hospitals and 78 percent of physicians' offices were using certified technology for health care records (Office of the National Coordinator for Health Information Technology, 2018). No longer in paper form, the digitized information opens opportunities for patients and clinicians to have a fuller and more timely picture of an individual's health and health care experience. Widespread availability of health data via EHRs has enabled more data-driven, team-based approaches to care coordination and patient-centric case management. However, to optimize our investment in health IT, information from multiple sources, devices, and organizations across the care continuum must be able to flow at the right time, to the right party, for the right patient.

Unfortunately, most EHRs, medical devices, and other IT systems are not interoperable—that is, they do not have the functional ability to "work with other systems or products without special effort on the part of the customer" (IEEE, 2016). In an elaborative variation of this definition, the 21st Century Cures Act of 2016 specifically defines an interoperable health IT system as one that "(a) enables the secure exchange of electronic health information with, and use of electronic health information from, other health information technology without special effort on the part of the user; (b) allows for complete access, exchange, and use of all electronically accessible health information for authorized use under applicable State or Federal law; and (c) does not constitute information blocking" (114th Congress, 2015).

Recent data indicate that fewer than one in three hospitals is able to electronically find, send, receive, and integrate patient information from another provider (*Figure 1*) (Holmgren, Patel et al., 2017). When patients experience a care transition

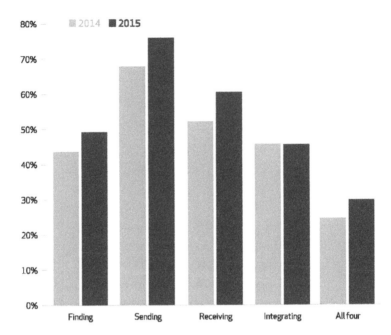

Percentages of US Hospitals with Interoperability in Four Core Domains, 2014 and 2015, Based on Data from the IT Supplement of the American Association Annual Survey

SOURCE: Reprint from Exhibit 1 from Holmgren et al. 2017. Progress in interoperability: Measuring US hospitals' engagement in sharing data. *Health Affairs* 36(10), 1820–1827.

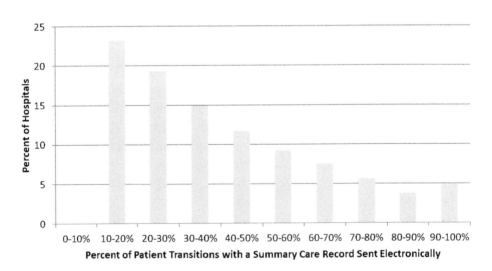

Percentages of Patient Transitions with a Summary Care Record Sent Electronically, Based on Hospital Attestations to Stage 2 of the Medicare Meaningful Use Program from September 2014 to April 2016

SOURCE: Reprint from Figure 2 in Lin et al. 2017. Technology, incentives, or both? Factors related to level of hospital health information exchange. *Health Services Research*.

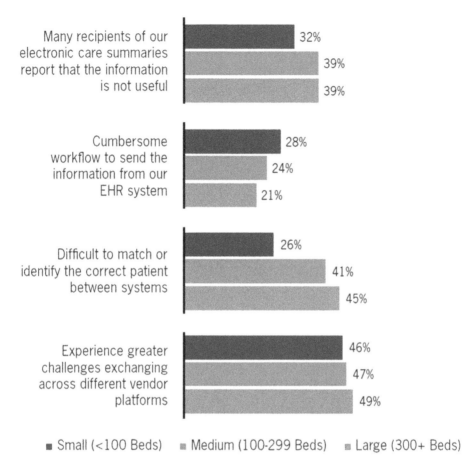

Barriers Experienced by Hospitals/Health Systems When Trying to Electronically Send, Receive, or Find Patient Health Information, by Bed Size, 2016/2017

SOURCE: American Hospital Association (AHA) Annual Survey Information Technology Supplement Data Brief March 2018, based on data collected from November 2016 to April 2017. © Used with permission of American Hospital Association.

such as discharges or referrals, most providers still rely on paper or fax to some extent when sending a care summary, potentially creating fragmentation in care coordination (*Figure 2*) (Lin, Everson et al., 2017). Of note, HITECH Act's stage 2 Meaningful Use program, which began in 2014, required hospitals to send the care record summaries electronically to the subsequent provider for a minimum of 10 percent of care transitions (Office of the National Coordinator for Health Information Technology, 2014). Although hospitals and health systems have increased sharing inside and outside of their organizations, many encounter barriers to data sharing and to using the shared data effectively (*Figure 3*) (American

Hospital Association, 2018). Some of these barriers are technical in nature, such as the format of the information transmitted, yet, equally if not more challenging barriers are socio-technical and relate to the integration of information into EHRs and clinician workflow to support decision making.

In addition to weak incentives, poor coordination, and other market barriers, suboptimal acquisition processes in the current marketplace also contribute to data silos and (unintended) blockage. Hospitals and other health care providers purchase systems and equipment from a variety of different manufacturers, and frequently, each comes with its own proprietary interface technology. As a result, most health care provider organizations spend time and money setting up each technology in a different way, instead of being able to rely on a consistent means of connectivity. Organizations often invest in separate proprietary "middleware" systems in efforts to connect disparate pieces of technology to feed data from bedside devices to EHRs, clinical registries, and other applications. Many bedside devices are unable to transmit data to other clinical IT systems and require manual transcription from one device or system to another. Nationwide, health systems must devote countless resources and personnel simply to dealing with the consequences of "non-interoperability" (West Health Institute 2013).

This environment has produced an entire market segment dedicated to health care integration technology. Vendors compete on solution effectiveness, driven by profitability and optimization for their customers, not necessarily aligned with patient interests or the industry as a whole. In the absence of standardized, shared solutions, proprietary software and hardware solutions remain common across the ecosystem. The resulting procurement "vendor lock" and reliance on makeshift workflow solutions perpetuates a culture that resists a transition to interoperability.

The lack of interoperability imposes an exhausting litany of clerical tasks for the clinical staff, contributing to staff burnout and waste (Cantwell and McDermott 2016). In addition to staff time spent on manually entering readings from a device (e.g., vital signs) onto paper or electronic charts (Hendrich, Chow et al., 2008), another common source of inefficiency is time spent manually programming devices (e.g., infusion pumps), a process that is often cumbersome and prone to error. These time burdens are also felt intensively by clinicians who have become responsible for a mix of documentation and reporting requirements that can add hours of extra work every day. Unlike in other industries where computerization has made work easier, deployment of EHRs in their current state—coupled with growing requirements for high-quality reporting and regulatory compliance—create additional work and exacerbate clinician burnout (Strongwater and Lee 2016). In addition, although EHRs have been widely adopted, essential areas for improvement remain, such as the inclusions of high-granularity measurements, waveforms, alarms, device alarm threshold or filter settings, and incomplete/erroneous data in EHRs partially attributable to manual entry (Weininger et al. 2016). Enhancing seamless exchanges of data as a means to improve data quality and minimize the need to rely on manual staff processes is recognized by the Office of the National Coordinator for Health Information Technology (ONC) as a core goal for reducing provider burden.

A report published by the West Health Institute in 2013 estimated that widespread medical device interoperability could eliminate at least $36 billion of waste in inpatient settings alone (West Health Institute, 2013). It was estimated that functional interoperability leads to increased efficiency, lower costs, and better quality of care through four primary drivers: reducing adverse events because of safety interlocks ($1.9 billion); reducing redundant testing ($1.5 billion); reducing clinician time spent manually entering information ($12 billion); and shortening length of stay through more timely transmission of critical information such as lab results ($18 billion).

Waste, inefficiency, and clinician burnout contribute to patient safety risk. Despite recent improvements in health care quality, preventable patient deaths and other adverse events still occur at an alarming rate. Medical errors result in as many as 3 million preventable adverse events each year, leading to as much as $17 billion in excess annual medical costs and nearly 100,000 deaths per year (Institute of Medicine, 2000; Jha et al. 2009). Although the proportion of patient harm that is directly attributable to the lack of interoperability is unknown, several common causes of medical errors, including drug errors, diagnostic errors, and failure to prevent injury, can partially be addressed by better data exchange among patients, medical devices, EHRs, consumer applications, and other health technology (Jha et al. 2009).

SUBOPTIMAL NATURE OF HEALTH CARE TECHNOLOGY PURCHASING

Although there are many technical, cultural, and political barriers that limit the progress toward system-wide interoperability, three main challenges stand out. First, despite the existence of certain health data standards, a common view of interoperability is lacking across health care systems. Second, in the absence of a harmonizing or coordinating body across health care systems, implementation of these standards is subject to interpretation, with minimal consistency across technology suppliers and health care organizations. Third, even if technical interoperability could be achieved, the practice of data blocking and data hoarding limits the flow of information.

Currently, procurement requirements and requests for proposals (RFPs) are generally based on narrow technical specifications of clinical use and regulatory guidance, reflecting the views of a small number of specialized end users or technical experts. Many health systems lack the technical and human resources required to create detailed specifications and to incorporate them into contracts on their own. Rather than purchasing an integrated suite of technologies, many health care organizations still acquire numerous individual "best-of-breed" IT modules to support specific workflow needs in areas such as operating rooms, intensive care units, and clinics.

Many organizations also face the conundrum of whether to upgrade a technology or device incrementally, or to acquire new systems with advanced functions to support emerging needs. Given financial constraints and past investment in existing technologies, especially the EHR, organizations tend to prioritize actions that contain costs and minimize workflow disruptions above everything else. To optimize long-term value in the procurement of medical technologies, purchasers need to consider multiple dimensions—life cycle costs, device functions, use cases, interoperability, safety, usability, effect on productivity, and more. It will become increasingly important not only to define purchasing requirements but also to develop a measurement framework for assessing progress and effectiveness. According to the National Quality Forum, "interoperability-sensitive" quality measures, such as patient and caregiver burden and care coordination, reflect the areas that must be addressed to provide a comprehensive understanding of interoperability and its effect on health processes and outcomes (National Quality Forum 2017).

In other large and complex industries, such as aviation, telecommunications, and banking, a high degree of interoperability is not only advantageous and desirable, but also essential. Many of these industries did not rely solely on standard-setting bodies but, in addition, drove the introduction of more interoperable systems by exerting their market power. In some circumstances, vendors identified and pursued interoperable solutions as a market opportunity, (e.g., Internet communication protocols, Bluetooth headsets, and digital camera memory cards). In other cases, purchasers and consumers worked together to require detailed data-exchange capabilities through contracts and purchasing agreements. This is, in part, why we can use our ATM card at virtually any bank in the world, plug a charger into any socket on the wall, and book or obtain the up-to-date departure and arrival status of any flight on any airline.

The lack of integration common throughout health care would be unacceptable on safety grounds alone in any other high-risk field. Imagine if commercial airplanes were designed like many hospitals today. If a plane's safety system was unable to obtain real-time input from the landing gear sensor to sound an alarm while trying to land without its wheels down, it would be considered a defect and a safety risk. In this case, the aircraft's builder would either require data sharing to remediate the error or get a new landing gear vendor; in health care, health systems accept vendor constraints and purchase the technology, accepting safety risks and higher costs. The aviation systems engineering approach reconciles interoperability by design and provides valuable lessons for health care and its critical mission to ensure safety.

The ability to collaborate and share information is essential for delivering higher-quality care and better outcomes at a lower cost. Health care organizations are uniquely positioned to accelerate interoperability through the use of a more disciplined process by which to procure technologies. Moreover, beyond the potential tragedy of lives lost, the longer health care systems delay in taking necessary steps to adopt and implement interoperable systems, the higher their exposure to legal and economic risk resulting from avoidable errors and adverse events.

Progress toward interoperability at the point of care delivery is especially needed. In contrast to the "plug-and-play" world of consumer electronics, where consumer demand has driven a convergence on a few standardized interfaces and platforms, health care providers have not collectively demanded a consistent means of interoperability (West Health Institute, 2013). As a result, many vendors use distinct proprietary and closed communication methods even among their own devices. Additionally, some standards are loosely specified, with a number of options for configuration, meaning that even devices that use similar standards are unable to communicate with each other without further customization. Another barrier is that many medical device interoperability standards and profiles are published without a reference implementation to ensure implementability and adoption. The cost of medical device integration, for example, integrating ventilators and physiologic monitors to the EHR, was estimated at as much as $6,500 to $10,000 per bed in one-time costs, plus as much as 15 percent in annual maintenance fees (Moorman, 2010). These investments represent a substantial undertaking for hospital systems already contending with operating margins of less than 3 percent on revenue of approximately $700,000 per bed, based on average length and cost of inpatient stays (Becker's Hospital CFO Report, 2011). Solving this lack of interoperability in health care requires solutions beyond common data standards. As demonstrated in other industries, enabling data liquidity across the health care continuum will require the creation of a vendor-neutral interoperability platform architecture that is modular, scalable, services based, and secure. In health care, this approach should be driven by health systems, the purchasers of technology, in partnership with the vendors.

IMPROVING OUTCOMES AND VALUE THROUGH INTEROPERABILITY-FOCUSED PROCUREMENT

Making interoperability a priority core and affordable requirement within the acquisition strategy speaks directly to the value and return on investment in health technology spending. Regardless of size and for-profit status, most health system leaders who acquire and upgrade IT solutions, devices, and data systems aim to achieve the following basic goals:

- Reduce medical errors and protect patient safety
- Ready and full access to records on patient health, health care, and progress
- Identify and better manage patients' risks to achieve the best outcome possible
- Ensure that patients and families are part of the care team
- Facilitate compliance with relevant rules, regulations, and contractual mandates
- Link to new data exchange partners, (e.g., technology, analytics, and social services)
- Automate data entry and reduce administrative burden
- Improve staff productivity and caregiver/clinician satisfaction
- Reduce cost, variation, and duplicated care
- Streamline relevant administrative workflow, including billing and quality reporting
- Ensure continuous quality improvement and learning

Health care organizations are therefore not just seeking the ability to transmit records electronically from point A to point B; they are looking for *clinically meaningful* interoperability that improves patient safety and workflow, enhances value, and enables person-centered care. Being able to construct a longitudinal patient record enables providers to care for the whole patient rather than a single diagnosis or episode. True person-centered interoperability has the potential to empower individuals to become partners in their health care, and allows for their ability to directly contribute to and receive data from the EHR. To ensure that health care dollars are spent in pursuit of a safer, more productive and more cost-effective system, interoperability must be a prime purchasing priority.

In this special publication, we explore an acquisition approach to health care technology integration whereby purchasers drive interoperability in the course of procuring new technologies or updating technologies already in use. The accompanying Technical Supplement provides further guidance, including an implementation framework for procuring interoperable systems (Appendix A, Section 1); an engineering tool to facilitate the interoperability identification process called N-squared diagram, which helps systematically document interactions among hardware, software, and people (Appendix A, Section 2); example interoperability specification language (Appendix A, Section 3); and lessons learned from the defense industry (Appendix A, Section 4). By focusing on an acquisition-based approach to promoting interoperability, we see an opportunity to help transform how the industry procures health IT that includes beneficial clinical interoperability capabilities that can lead to system-wide interoperability.

II.

INTEROPERABILITY IN THE HEALTH ECOSYSTEM

INTEROPERABILITY CONCEPTS AND TIERS

There are different aspects to interoperability, requiring different facilitative specifications depending on the interface, character, and needs. In addition to *technical interoperability*, in which standardized protocols are used to allow secure data transfer from one machine to another, the elements of syntactic, semantic, and organizational interoperability afford further interface functions to allow information to be exchanged and understood, and to inform (see *Figure 4*).

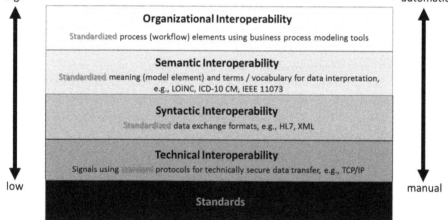

Levels of Health IT Interoperability

SOURCE: Based on Oemig F., and R. Snelick. 2016. *Healthcare interoperability standards compliance handbook* (p. 13, Figure 1.3). Switzerland: Springer.

NOTE: Data exchanges on the low technical level require more manual intervention to achieve the desired communication of meaning; data exchanges on the higher levels use more sophisticated standards, are more automatic, and require less manual intervention.

Syntactic interoperability brings standardized formats, such as the segments and elements in the HL7 Version 2 (v2) standard, for organizing the data in messages being exchanged. Specific kinds of data populate agreed-upon locations in the messages; for example, in an HL7 v2 laboratory results message, the third element of the observation/result (OBX-3) segment contains the identity of the lab test performed.

Semantic interoperability further enables more complete and specific data exchanges because an agreed-upon standard terminology is used by the data exchange partners. In the case of the lab test performed, the universal coding system LOINC (Logical Observation Identifiers Names and Codes) can be used to identify the lab test via a unique code name. For example, if the LOINC code *806–0* is in the third element of the OBX segment (OBX-3), the receiving system can automatically identify the test (i.e., leukocyte in cerebral spinal fluid by manual count) and process the rest of the message as the result of the leukocyte count.

Organizational interoperability involves the automation of workflow based on standardized business processes. In an HL7 v2 laboratory results message, for example, the eighth element of the OBX (OBX-8) segment indicates whether the result of the lab test performed is abnormal. If this element flags that the test result is outside of the normal range based on an agreed-upon clinical model, this flag can trigger a behavior in the receiving system, such as displaying an alert to the clinicians or ordering a follow-up lab test automatically.

When considered from the perspective of a health care delivery organization, *Figure 5* provides a conceptual model developed by William Stead from Vanderbilt University Medical Center and the Center for Medical Interoperability for assessing the maturity of data liquidity across multiple domains of interoperability. In this assessment, health system executives may assess organizational interoperability and data liquidity status by applying these five questions:

- Is the information your system needs to exchange properly formatted to meet your needs?
- Do the places that send and receive your data speak the same language?
- Is the information exchange sequenced to meet your needs?
- Do your information exchanges enable safety and optimal decisions?
- How connected, secure, and resilient is your health systems infrastructure?

Building on existing concepts of interoperability, the scope of interoperability covered in this report is holistic and based on the thesis that when interoperability is enabled throughout multiple levels in the health care ecosystem, the value of health technology investment can be maximized. Interoperability means the

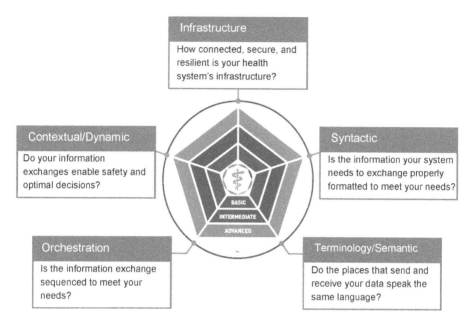

Interoperability Maturity Model
SOURCE: Center for Medical Interoperability, 2016.

ability to share, abstract, or link data from electronic health records, medical equipment, registries, laboratory results, records from prescriptions, and specialist consultations, as well as administrative and claims records, patient portals, even wearable and mobile devices. *Figure 6*, Panel A portrays the functional interoperability required across the three tiers: inter-facility (macro-tier), intrafacility (meso-tier), and point of care (micro-tier) in the health care ecosystem. It is important to note, however, that the three-tier structure represents an organizing schematic with some distinct features and stakeholders within each tier. In practice, data exchanges do and should occur across tiers. As the fully interoperable system envisioned in Figure 6, Panel B, interoperability needs to encompass all tiers to enable whole-person and whole-community care—(e.g., supporting population health management, data access by patients and families, and third-party application development, to name a few).

To illustrate the importance of all three tiers, consider a scenario where a patient is involved in a car accident. She is taken to the nearest county hospital and then needs to be transferred to a trauma center to undergo emergency surgery. The trauma center dispatches its ambulance to transport the patient. While en route, she experiences cardiac arrest. Even though the trauma center and the county hospital use different EHR vendors, the transport team and the trauma center are able to immediately obtain initial assessments, treatments, and imaging data. Meanwhile, the trauma center staff can see vital sign data from the ambulance in real time. Once the patient arrives at the trauma center, information from a variety of medical and monitoring devices is seamlessly integrated with information from the county hospital and displayed on a visual dashboard for the entire care team.

Or consider a health care system that has been increasingly engaged in value–based contracts with various payers through bundled payment or other

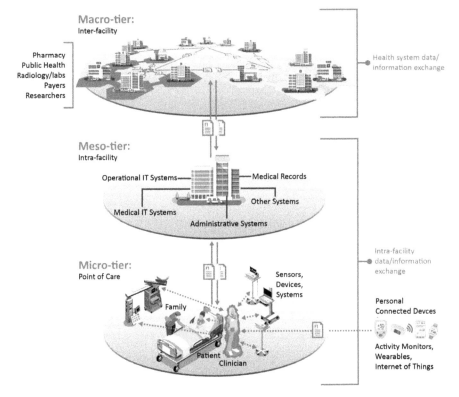

Interoperability in the Health Ecosystem—Inter-facility (Macro-), Intra-facility (Meso-), and Point-of-Care (Micro-) Tiers

Panel A. Tiers at which interoperability is required

NOTES: Despite some progress at the macro-tier, many providers still rely on paper or fax to some extent to exchange information with another facility and in cases where the data is exchanged digitally, it is often in CCDA format - an electronic replication of paper forms—which can be difficult for receiving clinicians to understand the patient's longitudinal care history. Within facilities (meso-tier) and at points of care (micro-tier), significant portions of data exchange depend on manual entry by clinical staff, which can adversely impact the timeliness, completeness, and accuracy of the data. Components of the health IT systems and healthcare devices may utilize proprietary interfaces to communicate or cannot automatically interoperate at all. There are very limited automated exchanges with personal connected devices.

SOURCE: Johns Hopkins University Applied Physics Lab, 2018

shared-risk programs. A care team designated to optimize care management for patients with diabetes needs to draw data from multiple record systems within the organization to monitor their hemoglobin A1c testing and control status, making sure the patients receive annual retinal examination, achieve blood pressure control, and receive medical attention for signs of nephropathy. They will also need data automatically integrated from multiple devices when the patients visit their primary care physicians, ultimately allowing patients to upload their own data from their mobile devices. Members of the care team can receive notifications nearly in real time when a patient is admitted to the

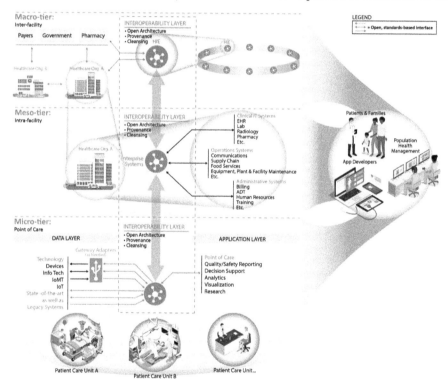

Panel B. Fully interoperable health and health care system

NOTES: Fast, secure, and seamless exchange of meaningful information for clinical decision making, care coordination, and patient engagement at the macro-, meso-, and micro-tiers. Through a standards-based, open architecture interoperability layer, care history and clinical workflows can be optimally integrated to support timely, seamless care. At the macro-tier, data exchanges across care providers, public health and social services allow patient-centered continuity of care. At the meso-tier, integrated IT infrastructure allows efficient workflow integration and risk management. At the micro-tier, connectivity through non-proprietary interfaces supports modular upgrades to plug-and-play components, as well as augmental in-person clinical encounters with telemedicine, mobile health technology, and patient portals. Across all tiers, open application programming interfaces (APIs) provide access to web and software developers to build tools that enable individual engagement and population health management.

SOURCE: Johns Hopkins University Applied Physics Lab, 2018

emergency department (ED). In addition, care coordinators rely on data shared from various external partners—ranging from pharmacies to behavioral health providers and social services agencies that serve the same patients—to provide high-value, high-quality, coordinated, and timely care. *Figure 6B* portrays this evolving state of interoperability, and related descriptions of the three tiers are described below and summarized in *Table 1*.

INTER-FACILITY (MACRO-TIER) INTEROPERABILITY

The macro-tier, illustrated in the top portion of *Figure 6*, represents health data exchanges across health care systems or between a health system and another entity such as a pharmacy or public health agency, some of which occur via regional or state-level Health Information Exchanges (HIEs) or an industry-wide network such as the Sequoia Project and the CommonWell Health Alliance. Over the past few years, the Patient Protection and Affordable Care Act and the Electronic Health Record Incentive (also known as the Meaningful Use) programs provided incentives to advance the basic ability to share data across health care systems. Information at this level is typically shared through the Clinical Document Architecture (CDA) framework, which enables clinical documents to be structured in a way that allows them to be read by both humans and computers.

Within each provider organization or health system, patient records are collated and made accessible through a centralized data aggregating and distribution entity (i.e., HIEs) and then shared across systems through information exchange gateways. Significant progress has been made in this tier, but the most recent data found that less than 30 percent of hospitals were able to find, send, receive, and integrate electronic patient information from outside providers (Holmgren, Patel et al., 2017). This means sizable challenges still exist: patient matching or identity management, fragmented records from multiple providers, attribution of the physician, and the potential for redundancy represent some of the usability and quality issues associated with data passed through the macro-tier. Providers and payers are also discovering new challenges in exchanging data outside the health care sector as they strive to address population health.

Here are three examples of macro-tier data exchange that are currently in play, though with significant gaps:

- *Intervention linkages.* In an effort to curtail prescription drug abuse, many states now employ a prescription drug monitoring program (PDMP), which tracks the prescribing and dispensing of controlled drugs such as opioids. Some HIEs also serve as an access point and data steward for interstate PDMP data sharing, as well as managing access from public health agencies and behavioral health providers.

- *Enterprise EHRs.* Obstetrical patients will typically see a clinician (e.g., physician or nurse midwife) in an ambulatory/office setting, deliver in a hospital or a freestanding birthing center, and return for postpartum care in the clinical office setting afterward. Depending on the health care system environment, these visits may be documented both within and outside of the enterprise EHR. Additionally, when an obstetrical patient encounters illnesses, injuries, or complications of pregnancy while traveling away from her primary location, it requires transmittal of laboratory and/or imaging studies along with clinical information and notes to properly inform her care.

- *Pooled data.* Many integrated health systems use a population health approach to prevent avoidable admissions or ED visits and to manage total cost of care. They partner with payers to unify claims and clinical data to drive population health insights at the point of care. These systems can benefit from the knowledge of any unplanned visits outside the health system (EDs or urgent care clinics), whether patient prescriptions were filled (from any pharmacy), whether patients with hypertension are achieving adequate control (measured in any clinic or community setting or even at home), whether patients received flu shots, patient-reported pain and activities after surgery, and many other clinical events.

INTRA-FACILITY (MESO-TIER) INTEROPERABILITY

The meso-tier in *Figure 6B* represents interoperability within a health care organization, in which information was exchanged between an EHR and other information management systems such as those used in clinical laboratories, pharmacies, food services, facility management, and patient administration (admission/discharge/transfer). Interoperability at this tier facilitates the operational workflow and coordination throughout the entire episode of care, supporting both clinical and administrative activities with a coherent picture of the patient's care processes and condition over time. Ensuring data elements are consistent across these systems not only reduces administrative burden but also improves patient experience with their care.

Currently, many hospitals procure locally hosted technologies such as pharmacy, laboratory, and other systems that enable varying degrees of integration with their respective EHR system. Some hospitals also acquire component technologies that aggregate data from these disparate IT systems before funneling that data to their EHR system for documentation of services and other purposes. Whether intra-facility interoperability is driven by individual health systems or through partnerships, the ability to exchange data among different health IT modules is typically provided through vendor-to-vendor agreements. Integration based on numerous unique, stand-alone agreements requires significant resource investment, technical expertise, and maintenance over each IT module's life cycle. This approach typically is not scalable, is costly, and is not sustainable as a long-term solution for the industry.

The following examples illustrate the value of enhancing meso-tier data exchange:

- Several hospitals deploy a central "command center" to monitor, streamline, and improve care efficiency. The dashboard used by the service- or system-level leadership requires linking a number of information management systems to provide a concise visual display of ambulance data, emergency department volumes, wait times, and bed status (full, empty, clean, and so on). In some instances, patient data from physiological monitors can be aggregated to provide predictive analytics to alert clinical staff about patients who may be under imminent risk for clinical deterioration. This information helps hospitals' managers reduce capacity uncertainties and optimize the efficiency of personnel and facility resources.

- A regional hospital system with a network of several tertiary care hospitals, specialty hospitals, and a dozen community-based facilities sought to streamline their required quality reporting activities across multiple governmental and private payers, meanwhile improving their quality measures and rankings. Using myocardial infarction outcomes as proof of concept, the head of the cardiology service requests weekly reporting of several core quality metrics pertaining to patients undergoing various forms of procedures: in-hospital mortality, readmissions, secondary prevention, and patient-reported outcomes. Until recently, much of the reporting was done manually. With enhanced interoperability across various systems within the organization, relevant data can now be automatically pulled from EHRs, ADT (admissions/discharge/transfer) records, lab systems, pharmacy, and radiology to populate an electronic quality and outcomes report on a weekly basis.

POINT-OF-CARE (MICRO-TIER) INTEROPERABILITY

The micro-tier represents the data and information exchanged at the point of patient care (*Figure 6*)—whether at a particular care site (e.g., equipment and monitors in an intensive care unit) or generated by patients themselves (e.g., wearable or mobile health applications). Interoperability within this tier has great potential for improving patient safety, reducing medical errors, and reducing costs; it is also the level at which health systems have significant control and accountability through their procurement processes. At the point of care, data streams may be quite disparate and heterogeneous, ranging from verbal communications to medical record entries, device settings, image data, traditional laboratory results (e.g., blood type), and nontraditional data such as genomics and other patient-specific data. As with the other tiers, the data can consist of a combination of structured data, unstructured data, free text, and verbal communications.

Currently, micro-tier data exchange still largely relies on clinical staff (*Figure 6, Panel A*). Data generated by a medical device that are not exported to other systems means clinical staff must interpret the data, manually transcribe relevant values into the medical record, and possibly initiate an adjustment to the course of treatment. Transcription errors are common; one study found an error rate as high as 19 percent when clinical staff manually transcribe vital signs onto paper and then subsequently enter them into EHR (Fieler et al. 2013). In comparison, the use of electronic vital signs documentation systems resulted in significantly fewer errors and shorter elapsed time. The lack of true interoperability at the point of care, coupled with the advances in medical technologies that make clinical decision making increasingly complex, puts a tremendous burden on providers and poses great risk of medical errors and eventually, patient harm.

For example:

- A cancer patient's patient-controlled analgesia (PCA) pump was programmed to maintain a low constant infusion rate of opioid but also respond to inputs from the patient. Currently, clinical staff would manually program the PCA pump while periodically monitoring combined dosage and pulse oximetry readings to detect potential respiratory depression. In the event of respiratory depression, staff would manually discontinue the infusion. An improved state of interoperability could include a PCA safety interlock that allows signals from a vital signs monitoring device to trigger a stop of the opioid infusion at the onset of respiratory depression.
- An academic health center sought to implement a number of "checklists" to prevent common harms experienced by intensive care unit patients, including harm from receiving disrespectful care and harm from receiving care that is not consistent with patient goals. Even though algorithms exist to predict a patient's risk for certain types of harm (e.g., based on vital signs, care history,

disease severity, and comorbidity), available technology has not provided an automated visual display of the conformity of a care regimen to recommended protocols. To fill this gap, researchers at Johns Hopkins Medicine (Romig, Tropello et al., 2015) used a systems engineering approach and developed a technology platform that integrated a variety of data elements from the EHR and from other sensor devices, which then graphically displayed the data on a tablet in real time to trigger and monitor the implementation of patient harm prevention measures.

Definitions, applications, and the current state of interoperability

	INTER-FACILITY EXCHANGE (MACRO-TIER)	INTRA-FACILITY EXCHANGE (MESO-TIER)	POINT OF CARE EXCHANGE (MICRO-TIER)
Definition	Exchange of information among organizations and networks.	Exchange of information among care units within an organization or network, including operations and administrative IT systems.	Point-of-care exchange at which care devices, equipment, records, and clinical staff interact with patients.
Example Clinical Applications	Continuity of care across different providers and types of facilities (e.g., providers in different geographical areas, multiple pharmacies); population health management in accountable care models through addressing medical, behavioral, and social needs; information exchange with public health agencies.	Consolidation and automatic exchange of patient records across laboratory and radiology with EHR; data exchanges among scheduling, billing, quality reporting, and care delivery IT systems; continuity of care across facilities within the network (e.g., outpatient clinics, EDs, in-patient services, and postacute care facilities).	Automatic data exchanges from bedside monitors to the EHR; programmable infusion pumps with safety interlock that allow signals from patient vital signs monitors; postdischarge patient monitoring through wearable devices.
Current State	Some progress in data exchange standards, regional HIEs, and direct exchanges across providers. Challenges remain in workflow integration.	Some progress through software interfaces, but manual handling and duplication of records are common.	Clinical staff performs the majority of data exchange. Adoption of custom middleware solutions to enable connections between two proprietary interfaces.
Future State	Fast and secure data exchanges across care providers; coordinated data aggregation across clinical, behavioral health, public health, and social service agencies in support of population health management; access and control by patients for their own care record.	Integrated IT infrastructure within the health care provider systems that allow seamless application of risk management analytics, workflow integration, quality improvement and reporting, and cybersecurity protection.	Integrated patient care devices and IT system based on open architecture connectivity and nonproprietary standards; modular upgrades to plug-and-play components and devices as needed; integrated telemedicine capabilities, connected mobile health technology, and patient portals to augment in-person clinical encounters.

Currently, medical device vendors lack the market imperative to ensure interoperability, partly because providers bear most of the costs of integrating these devices and because there is an absence of an aligned demand to drive change in the technology ecosystem. Some health care providers achieve some level of medical device integration, particularly to support data to EHR integration. However, in the perceived absence of a prominent value proposition, many devices are not integrated with other technologies at all. Although it is unlikely that medical device and IT vendors will spontaneously and proactively move toward standardized "plug-and-play" device interoperability, clearly clinicians have significant motivation for demanding medical device data liquidity and interoperability. Solutions are urgently needed to address the efficiency, capacity, and cost issues faced by health care providers under the pressure to shift toward value-based payment models.

CURRENT STATE IN PRACTICE

The community of health IT vendors has evolved primarily into two categories: companies that support the ambulatory market, and those targeting the hospital market. There was initially little crossover between these two groups, but more recently, vendors have moved toward providing health IT solutions capable of functioning in both domains. Health IT solutions for the in-patient setting are more complex, and far fewer vendors service that market, which is dominated by Epic Systems, Cerner, and MEDITECH. The market is also segmented by size and complexity; academic medical centers and large integrated delivery networks select vendors that are different from those selected by small critical access hospitals. For smaller or independent practices, less expensive or less resource-intensive platforms such as athenahealth and eClinicalWorks lead in market share. This breakdown is evolving, however, as large EHR vendors have been retooling their offerings to be more competitive in different market segments.

In contrast, as indicated in *Figure 7*, the ambulatory market is characterized by a much larger number of vendors (684 as of July 2017) with Epic again demonstrating significant market share, followed by Allscripts and eClinicalWorks. Nevertheless, the amount of consolidation and the number of developers leaving the market is increasing. This trend creates difficulty for individual physicians and small practices that lack the infrastructure support to make transitions to an alternative vendor, which can be time consuming and costly, and provide an opportunity for clinical errors. Of note, recognizing the need, the ONC developed technical support resources targeted at smaller providers within its Health IT Playbook

(Office of the National Coordinator for Health Information Technology,) and the EHR Contracting Guide (Office of the National Coordinator for Health Information Technology, 2016). Finally, an increasing percentage of users are choosing to have their data hosted in a secure cloud by their vendors. The vendor provides the security, infrastructure, backup, and maintenance of the software and data that many find difficult to manage in small practice settings. In addition, cloud-based technologies are much easier and less costly to update.

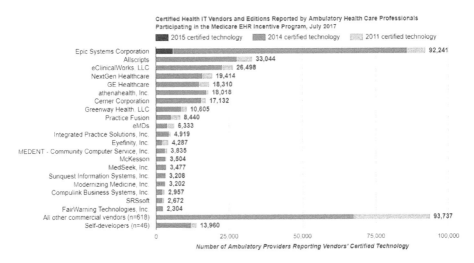

Certified Health IT Vendors and Editions Reported by Ambulatory Health Care Professionals Participating in the Medicare EHR Incentive Program, July 2017

2015 certified technology   2014 certified technology   2011 certified technology

Epic Systems Corporation	92,241
Allscripts	33,044
eClinicalWorks, LLC	26,498
NextGen Healthcare	19,414
GE Healthcare	18,310
athenahealth, Inc.	18,018
Cerner Corporation	17,132
Greenway Health, LLC	10,605
Practice Fusion	8,440
eMDs	6,333
Integrated Practice Solutions, Inc.	4,919
Eyefinity, Inc.	4,287
MEDENT - Community Computer Service, Inc.	3,835
McKesson	3,504
MedSeek, Inc.	3,477
Sunquest Information Systems, Inc.	3,208
Modernizing Medicine, Inc.	3,202
Compulink Business Systems, Inc.	2,957
SRSsoft	2,672
FairWarning Technologies, Inc.	2,304
All other commercial vendors (n=618)	93,737
Self-developers (n=46)	13,960

Number of Ambulatory Providers Reporting Vendors' Certified Technology

Health IT Vendors

Certified Health IT Developers and Editions Reported by Ambulatory Primary Care Physicians, Medical and Surgical Specialists, Podiatrists, Optometrists, Dentists, and Chiropractors Participating in the Medicare EHR Incentive Program

SOURCE: Office of the National Coordinator for Health IT. July 2017. https://dashboard.healthit.gov/quickstats/pages/FIG-Vendors-of-EHRs-to-Participating-Professionals.php.

With broad recognition of the importance and value of interoperability in health care, various governmental and industry entities have collectively made progress across all three tiers of interoperability. What follows are some exemplary national and consortium efforts:

- A 2005 report by the Commission on Systemic Interoperability identified a set of 14 recommendations in a multidimensional approach to achieve connectivity, privacy, and security (Commission on Systemic Interoperability, 2005).
- A 2009 consensus study by the National Research Council advocates rebalancing the portfolio of investments in health care IT to provide greater support for health care providers, patients, and family caregivers as well as observing

proven principles for success in designing and implementing IT to advance patient safety (National Research Council, 2012).

- A 2010 report by the President's Council of Advisors on Science and Technology (PCAST) issued the first clear statement that interoperability needed to be designed into the technical infrastructure from the beginning, in contrast to an ad hoc effort at the interface between components (President's Council of Advisors on Science and Technology, 2010).
- Funded by the ONC, a 2013 report by the independent JASON advisory group highlighted the lack of an architecture supporting standardized application programming interfaces (APIs), as well as EHR vendor technology and business practices, as structural impediments to achieving interoperability (JASON 2013). The report recommended a centrally orchestrated interoperability architecture based on open APIs and advanced intermediary applications and services. The 2014 JASON Task Force report affirmed such an architectural approach and further mapped existing standards to the architecture (JASON Report Task Force, 2014).
- Integrating the Healthcare Enterprise (IHE) is an initiative started in 1997 by health care industry professionals with the initial goal of improving the integration of imaging data into hospital IT infrastructure. Since then, IHE has expanded its scope to include multiple functional domains (e.g., laboratory, cardiology, and pathology), which create specific integration profile documents and provide guidance on the coordinated use of established standards such as Digital Imaging and Communication in Medicine (DICOM) and Health Level Seven International (HL7) (Rhoads, Cooper et al., 2009).
- The Medical Device Innovation Consortium (MDIC) is a public-private partnership formed in 2012 to advance medical device regulatory science for patient benefit. Its membership includes representatives of the U.S. Food and Drug Administration (FDA), National Institutes of Health (NIH), Centers for Medicare and Medicaid Services (CMS), industry, and nonprofits and patient organizations. In addition to developing regulatory science tools to support clinical trial innovation and incorporating patient engagement, MDIC also established the National Evaluation System for health Technology (NEST) coordinating center to enhance interoperability efforts by making device data available.
- The Center for Medical Interoperability (CMI) is a nonprofit organization founded in 2013 as a cooperative research and development lab. CMI membership is limited to health systems, individuals, and self-insured corporations but works with a variety of stakeholders. CMI aims to provide centralized engineering resources in enabling vendor-neutral, plug-and-play interoperability

in the form of specifications, software reference implementations, and an interoperability testing and certification program.

- ONC Interoperability Standards Advisory: First established in 2015 and updated annually, the ONC interoperability standards advisory provides guidance on "best-of-breed" data exchange standards, integration profiles, and implementation guides based on intended purpose (i.e., use cases), maturity, and degree of adoption. Although the advisory's structure and content is most amenable to aiding system and device developers in solving specific data exchange issues, it is a useful reference for interoperability "customers" working to develop procurement specifications.

- The Argonaut Project is a private-sector initiative to advance industry adoption of modern, open interoperability standards. The purpose of the Argonaut Project is to accelerate time to market by developing a first-generation Fast Healthcare Interoperability Resources (FHIR)-based APIs (see Appendix, Box A1-3) and Core Data Services specification to enable expanded information sharing for EHRs and other health IT. This effort follows on recommendations from the JASON Task Force Report.

- Since 2012, the nonprofit Sequoia Project organization has taken over the management of the eHealth Exchange, now the largest health information exchange network in the country. The Sequoia Project also operates the Carequality initiative, which facilitates technical and policy agreements to enable nationwide interoperability among diverse representatives of payers, EHR vendors, accountable care organizations, record locator service providers, and other existing networks. The Carequality interoperability framework provides the legal terms, policy requirements, technical specifications, and governance processes to bridge networks and services. In parallel, CommonWell Health Alliance is a nonprofit trade association of health IT companies to create universal access to health data. In 2016, CommonWell and Carequality announced enhanced collaboration and expanded connectivity, with an immediate focus on extending providers' ability to request and retrieve medical records electronically. Together, the CommonWell framework and Carequality network represent more than 90 percent of the acute care EHR market and nearly 60 percent of the ambulatory EHR market, including 15,000 hospitals, clinics, and other health care organizations. Both Sequoia and CommonWell partner with the Argonaut Project to enable more comprehensive FHIR-based exchange at scale.

- The 21st Century Cures Act was enacted in December 2016 and, in part, included provisions to enhance interoperability and eliminate information blocking, defined broadly as a "practice that . . . is likely to interfere with, prevent, or materially discourage access, exchange or use of electronic health information." The act calls for, "without special efforts," open APIs based on modern standards such as JSON and FHIR. In addition, the act requires the federal government to develop a Trusted Exchange Framework and Common Agreement (TEFCA) to provide a single "on-ramp" to nationwide interoperability while achieving a competitive, sustainable market (114th Congress, 2015).

Taken together, these milestone efforts pave the way toward better interoperability on several fronts: the development of data exchange standards, promoting open API, combating information blocking, building data partnerships with the social services sector and public health, embracing open platform and exchange capabilities at the delivery system level, and integrating claims, EHR, and pharmacy data.

III.

INTEROPERABILITY PROCUREMENT SPECIFICATION STRATEGIES

D rawing on the lessons of other industries and using a systems engineer-ing approach, the initial priority for both manufacturers and health care organizations is the identification of the goals for the product being acquired, followed by a disciplined process for acquiring the product. In principle, only after functional requirements and design specifications of the product have been listed should decisions be made about which technologies to include. Interoperability should be a functional requirement.

The process of establishing requirements first necessitates a clear definition of the clinical use cases and needs, which include all aspects of capability, per-formance, process, and workflow. A needs statement should articulate what the user is attempting to accomplish as well as how this capability relates to the broader mission. In other words, the requirements should state *what* the health IT products must be able to do, expressed as desired outcomes for health IT interoperability (e.g., producing required clinical quality metrics, decision support, safety interlocks) (Medical Device Plug-and-Play Interoperability & Cybersecurity [MD PnP] Program at Massachusetts General Hospital, 2018), as well as *how* the health IT module uses various data exchange standards (e.g., Clinical Document Architecture [CDA], Application Programming Interfaces [APIs], or other standards that support clinical information exchange). Several organizations such as IHE and HL7 provide free resources, including use cases, integration profiles, and implementation guides that can help organizations delineate the scope, capabilities, desired outcomes, and potential limitations. *Box A1-1* in Appendix A describes them in more detail.

Once user needs are defined, the next layer of technical requirements should be derived from those user needs. Requirements may include functional require-ments, including interoperability, and other operational requirements or constraints such as timeliness and accuracy. Once the requirements have been derived from the user needs, they must be articulated in contracting documents to minimize ambiguity. The onus then falls on the industry supplier of the system or capability to demonstrate their compliance with the open architecture required to support industry standards and specifications in the contract.

For example, a hospital upgrading their laboratory information system (LIS) may require interoperability between the hospital's legacy EHR system and the new laboratory system. The RFP may include language such as, "The vendor's LIS shall receive laboratory orders from a legacy EHR system that is compliant with the HL7 Version 2.5.1 Implementation Guide: S & I Framework Laboratory Orders from EHR, release 1 DSTU Release 2—US Realm." Another hospital that aims to procure an open architecture interoperability platform to integrate a set of patient care devices to pass data directly to the EHR system may include language such as, "The *open architecture interoperability platform* shall receive data from the device types and manufacturers listed in Table X . . . products that provide the option of communicating with the highlighted device types in Table Y in compliance with IHE PCD DEC Optimized Exchange Protocol will be ranked higher as described in section Z." (See Appendix A Technical Supplement, Section 3.)

Additional sample language specification with corresponding applications, as well as sample language for modular open systems architecture (further discussed below) and an open business model can be found in Appendix A, Section 3.

Interface standards, given the lack of a centralized authority, must be leveraged across organizations. To achieve this, each institution must provide guidance and a strategy—in the form of a long-range road map—to enable the organization to meet its objectives and to allow for cross-organizational sharing of interface standards. Accounting for needed organizational resources is, of course, imperative—including not only dedicated budget and human resources to assess, select, and implement interoperable solutions, but a process to obtain and train interoperability enablers within the organization.

MODULAR OPEN SYSTEMS ARCHITECTURE

The concept of Modular Open Systems Architecture (MOSA) is prevalent throughout this holistic view. By definition, an open system architecture is "organized decomposition, using carefully defined execution boundaries, layered onto a framework of software and hardware shared services and a vibrant business model that facilitates competition." (Guertin and Hurt, 2013, page iii). An expedient way to determine whether a system employs an open system is to ask, "Can one or more qualified third parties add, modify, replace, remove, or provide support for a component of a system, based on open standards and published interfaces for the component of that system?" (Guertin and Hurt, 2013, page viii).

A modular open systems architecture embodies five features:

1. Modular design standards that allow for independent acquisition of plug-and-play components;
2. Enterprise investment strategies, based on collaboration and trust, that maximize reuse of proven hardware system designs and ensure health care organizations spend the least to get the best;
3. Transformation of the life cycle sustainment strategies for software intensive systems through proven technology insertion and software product upgrade techniques;
4. Lower development risk through transparency of system designs and continuous design disclosure; and
5. Strategic use of data rights to ensure a level playing field and access to alternative solutions and sources across the life cycle.

The US military is one of the pioneers in adopting such a model as a broad strategic choice. *Box 1* describes the lessons learned from transitioning to the requirement-driven acquisition at the Department of Defense military health system. Two additional case studies (Appendix A Technical Supplement, Section 4) detail the processes undertaken by the US Navy, which enabled more open and modular procurement models for its submarines and unmanned ground vehicle system.

Incubating a wide adoption of such modular open system architecture across the macro-, meso-, and micro-tiers requires many external factors: the existence of independent organization(s) to specify technical standards for data exchange

BOX 1

Requirement-Driven Acquisition at the Department of Defense: Lessons Learned

The Military Health System (MHS), a $50 billion-per-year enterprise, is a unique and vital part of US health care and national defense. With the goal of providing Better Care, Better Health, Increased Readiness, and Lower Cost to almost 10 million service members, dependents, and military retirees, the MHS offers comprehensive medical services, to include trauma care in austere environments, preventive medicine, and other health services across diverse patient populations and conditions.

In addition to providing world-class health care, the MHS is a pioneer in the use of automation to improve enterprise-wide health and health care outcomes. In 2013, the Department of Defense (DoD) sought to improve health information exchange across the MHS by procuring a commercial-off-the-shelf (COTS) EHR system to foster interoperability, standardization, and cybersecurity across the MHS's electronic platform. To that end, MHS GENESIS, a Cerner Millennium product, is being deployed to 55 hospitals and more than 350 clinics, as well as numerous military operational platforms across the MHS. In addition to advancing interoperability between DoD, the Department of Veterans Affairs (VA), and private-sector providers, MHS GENESIS advances interoperability within the walls of military hospitals—prompting a change in the procurement strategy for medical and end-user devices within the military treatment facilities. MHS GENESIS has been configured to meet the DoD cybersecurity requirements, which has become a major driver for interoperability among components of the record system and medical devices. When the MHS turns to the commercial marketplace, it will scrutinize every aspect of health care delivery for devices and equipment that meet these goals for interoperability—integration with the MHS GENESIS EHR, integration between other medical devices, and the DoD's security framework. The opportunity before the MHS to drive interoperability, efficiency, and better patient service goes beyond procuring the EHR to include a gateway to medical devices that "talk" to the EHR and to one another.

The Defense Health Agency's (DHA's) approach to interoperability creates functionally based acquisition requirements that can serve as a pivotal opportunity for the MHS and other health programs to influence the market behavior of health care vendors. Specifically, MHS requirements for medical devices that meet EHR interoperability and cybersecurity requirements, combined with the purchasing power of DHA, the military services, and the VA, could drive the marketplace toward competitive device development and pricing. Should federal agencies such as the VA and Indian Health Service join those efforts—as the VA already has with its decision to acquire the same commercial product on which MHS GENESIS is based—federal health programs will be in a position to drive the market toward responsiveness to these needs, not just in military or VA hospitals, but for providers across the country.

The primary goal of MHS GENESIS, as with all MHS endeavors, is to provide Better Care, Better Health, Increased Readiness, and Lower Cost to our beneficiaries. By maximizing EHR interoperability and building cybersecurity requirements into its acquisition model, MHS can bring a positive influence to the marketplace in ways that drive the right incentives and product improvements to benefit the entire MHS, US health care, and national defense.

SOURCE: Raquel C. Bono, US Department of Defense, 2017

(technical, syntactic, semantic, and operational, *Figure 4*); a vendor-neutral reference architecture based on open architecture principles offered to multiple industry integrators for commercialization; multiple "integrators" capable of producing modules (or components within a module) that adhere to the technical standards for data exchange and the detailed reference architecture; certification bodies to ensure compliance to standards; and a framework to evaluate the "maturity" of interoperability that specific devices, systems, and/or clinical domains have achieved. One example is the CMI Interoperability Maturity Model described earlier (*Figure 5*), which provides a mechanism by which to analyze the requirements of a situation and match it with the optimal level of interoperability along a number of dimensions: infrastructure, syntactic, terminology/semantic, conversational complexity, and contextual/dynamic. While the field as a whole continues to evolve toward this vision, health technology purchasers can take strategic steps today to enhance interoperability and optimize their investment in health IT.

FRAMEWORK FOR PROCURING SYSTEMS THAT ARE PROGRESSIVELY INTEROPERABLE

Fundamentally, driving system-wide interoperability requires more than technical resources and competencies; it also requires alignments of culture, governance structure, and a viable and sustainable business model. For an individual hospital system, the institution's leadership must start by prioritizing interoperability as mission critical, as well as by providing a carefully built accountability structure to execute, maintain, and continuously improve. In addition, to incrementally improve connectivity of new technology acquisitions, continuous improvement involves versioning and backward compatibility checks. Recognition that interoperability must be managed as a component of a long-term business strategy rather than as numerous uncoordinated, one-off purchase decisions must permeate individual organizations and the entire health care sector. Collectively and over time, the health IT industry and health care providers require a shared understanding that data liquidity and openness must be the norm, not the exception. Conformance testing and certification requirements are also essential shared infrastructure for the field at large.

Specifically, the steering committee identified five priorities for health care organization and system leader action:

1. **COMMIT: Declare interoperability a primary priority and form an organization-wide interoperability steering group or related capacity to champion the IT acquisition strategy.**

Each health system leader should articulate how enhancing interoperability is key to the organization's mission as health care providers and emphasize the priority of purchasing strategies to achieve these goals. By identifying stakeholders and enablers within the organization, forming an interoperability steering group (or a working group with related capacity within the existing steering committee), health systems can create the clear governance structure to develop, oversee, and sustain a long-term road map toward interoperability that can continuously improve technology procurement driven by end-user needs and adapt to industry-wide best practices. (See Appendix A Technical Supplement.)

2.   **IDENTIFY: Charge this group with identifying the set of interoperability goals, requirements, and model use cases for the procurement process to deliver on organizational priorities and patient outcome goals.**

Health care organizations must rethink how disparate health IT modules are connected, not just within one hospital, but also among every entity involved in a patient's care, including physicians' offices, home health agencies, other postacute-care facilities, and social services. With strong engagement from the organization's interoperability steering group, health system leaders should define their strategic priority and goals for interoperability in various clinical interactions and applications on an annual basis. The interoperability steering group should also oversee the identification of key clinical use cases that bear the highest urgency for improvement in interoperability and require strategic technology acquisition. Guided by a road map charting the path toward a modular open system architecture model, these priorities should reflect direct linkages to the organization's overall strategic planning process for quality improvement as well as for technology acquisition and management. (See Appendix A Technical Supplement, Section 1.) Because not all organizations will have internal capacity to write detailed specifications, work in this arena should be openly and freely shared among health care organizations, vendors, and researchers (see below).

3.   **COLLABORATE: Create a sector-wide strategy and partner with other sector stakeholders to align on common contracting requirements and specifications for the next generation of interoperable health IT.**

Health system leaders should assertively collaborate with other health care providers, payers, and vendors to form a shared vision for digital interoperability and shared resources for procuring health IT. In addition to ad hoc strategic partnerships, a national coordinated initiative should be launched to create a shared "commons" that includes basic requirement specifications for trust, common data elements and definitions, data security, connectivity, timeliness, accuracy, and usability to clinicians and patients. Such alignment can then be realized over time by embracing a clearly defined procurement strategy and demanding that these specifications be met. As part of this effort, a public platform test bed or a certification body should be established that allows for low-cost access to connectivity testing for providers and developers of all sizes and resource levels. Through collaboration and coordination, the purchasers of health care technology can benefit from more efficient acquisition, while the marketplace becomes more competitive and encouraging to innovations.

4. **SPECIFY: Use the collaboratively developed specifications to state clear, functional interoperability requirements in existing and future proposals and contracts.**

Each health system leader should mandate that the interoperability steering group build institutional capacity to provide clear, unambiguous technical specifications on high-priority IT acquisitions and upgrades. In many industries, such specifications often span hundreds of pages and provide detailed information to avoid vendor latitude in interpreting requested data exchange and other plug-and-play standards. Health systems should leverage existing and emerging resources to translate their interoperability needs into procurement specification language, but doing so takes institutional commitment of will and resources. (See Appendix A Technical Supplement, Section 1.)

5. **ASSESS: Establish and monitor short-term and long-term metrics for the progress and contributions of interoperability to system-wide learning and improvement of health outcomes.**

Each health system leader should define the desired end-state and key performance indicators related to interoperability across the macro-, meso-, and micro-tiers. At the organizational level, metrics that demonstrate the short-term and long-term value from acquiring the right technology portfolio through achieving their articulated quality, outcome, and cost goals should be developed and monitored over time. From the business infrastructure standpoint, there should be an accompanying data dimension for each of the three tiers that centers on allowable use cases for data sharing at a business level beyond how each device on the system can communicate.

In accordance with the five action priorities for interoperability—Commit, Identify, Collaborate, Specify, and Assess—several organizational steps are common elements:

- **An interoperability steering group:** This team, with the CEO's direct engagement, serves as the organizational champion that motivates the procurement framework toward interoperability and system openness and guides the procurement decisions and specifications. The group should include diverse representatives within the health care organization (e.g., clinical, engineering, administrative, business, operations, supply chain, and IT) and be responsible for staying abreast of advances in interoperability and open systems, developing objectives and a long-range interoperability road map, identifying interoperability and data security requirements, translating requirements to procurement specifications, and measuring return on investment.
- **Long-range interoperability road map:** The road map is a component of the organization's multiyear procurement plan that pursues the vision for system openness and interoperability with incremental objectives and guideposts. The interoperability steering group should update the road map annually to reflect organizational or market changes that influence procurement priorities.
- **Interoperability needs identification process:** The interoperability steering group should engage key stakeholders internally to identify needs and opportunities for enhanced interoperability in its care processes. This means documenting and visualizing the complex information and workflow interactions in a health care setting and the translation of these interactions to interoperability needs for new or upgraded health IT systems. Data security and privacy protection needs should be identified as part of the process. The N-square diagram, one of the tools routinely used in systems engineering for tabulating interactions between hardware and/or software systems, may facilitate this process (see Appendix A Technical Supplement, Section 2).
- **Interoperability procurement specification process:** The interoperability steering group should lead the translation of interoperability needs to procurement specifications in RFPs by leveraging various data exchange standards, supporting resources, and existing reference architecture. The ONC Interoperability Standards Advisory provides some useful resources, including best practice guidance on data exchange standards, production of security and patient privacy, implementation guides, and integration profiles as well as guidance on contracting with EHR vendors (Office of the National Coordinator for Health Information Technology, 2016).

Depending on the size of the organization and the resources at hand, the prerequisite elements proposed here may vary in their scale and vigor. Nevertheless, executives in every health care organization should ensure all four elements are present as part of a long-term capacity and infrastructure-building strategy. The Technical Supplement, in Appendix A, provides more detailed guidance for developing each element within health systems.

CONTRACTING AND MANAGING VENDORS THROUGH REQUESTS FOR PROPOSAL (RFPs)

Once the steering group, road map, and appropriate needs and resources have been identified within a health care organization or network, the detailed procurement strategy must also be developed and implemented. This includes describing the organization's interoperability requirements in any contractual RFPs and selecting those vendor solutions that meet these requirements. It is also important to certify that the delivered system or component meets the requirements before acceptance. A common approach for a vendor is to offer its services to provide the subsystem integration. Although this can be an attractive option, it is critical for the purchaser to ensure that the vendor's interoperability expertise and commitment are not limited to that vendor's products; otherwise, the health care organization risks becoming "locked in" to one vendor. An alternative is to select an independent integration agent who would ensure cross-vendor interoperability. This approach allows modularity in the system so that new capabilities can easily be added in the future without relying on one vendor's solutions.

As part of the procurement process, metrics and measurements must be included for acceptance and functionality testing. Many use cases can be defined in the requirements specification with a clear listing of expected outcomes (including interoperability). Test scripts must be created to verify that the requirements are met, including steps that verify interoperability standards. The usefulness of conformance and interoperability testing tools depends not only on the quality of available standards, but also on the rigor of a sustained practice that continuously identifies relevant standards and reduces ambiguity. Such practice forms an imperative business infrastructure—it requires a dedicated team of people (an interoperability advisory committee) with an adequate mix of technical and clinical expertise, a structured process (e.g., the N-squared diagram), and a road map to achieve the end state. In many industries that achieved interoperability, that end state reflects some form of modular, open system architecture, where many IT components can be standardized and commoditized so that replacing and updating over time becomes easier for the health care providers.

The accompanying Technical Supplement (Appendix A) provides tools and terminology intended to facilitate such a process. It has four parts: Section 1 describes an overarching framework and implementation strategy for purchasing interoperable systems, including a step-by-step procurement specification process for organizations to follow when purchasing interoperable technology and guidance for making procurement decisions at each interoperability tier. Section 2 describes the application of the N-squared diagram, a systems engineering tool routinely used in the space and military sectors, to organize complex interactions among hardware and software systems. This prototypical approach represents an exemplary strategy to systematically identify and prioritize interoperability needs. Section 3 provides examples of interoperability specification language for several use cases. Section 4 describes two relevant case studies from nonhealthcare settings within the defense industry that have engaged similar interoperability challenges.

Looking ahead, each institution should not only take initiatives and overcome inertia to drive purchasing strategies internally but also actively drive interoperability among organizations at the macro-tier. In addition to building the technical infrastructure, health system leaders should recognize and pursue an overall business infrastructure that allows for more assertive procurement practices. More importantly, active collaboration among health care leaders is key to driving the entire health IT market toward interoperability at all three levels, as well as seamless interfaces with the rapidly expanding tools for individuals, families, and communities.

IV.

TRANSFORMING THE HEALTH IT MARKETPLACE

Smarter procurement of interoperable health IT—including both the technical architecture and the business infrastructure—is not only necessary to help solve quality and workflow challenges today, but also crucial for surviving and thriving in the rapidly changing health care landscape. As in most sectors, health care delivery is undergoing rapid changes, on both the data and the consumer fronts (Brigham and Johns, 2012; Flores et al. 2013). New data streams—structured and unstructured—are cascading into the health care realm from fitness devices, genetics and genomics, social media, and public health sources. Aggregating and processing such an explosive growth of data to allow predictive insight—through machine learning and clinical decision support, for instance—can provide timely, evidence-based, and customized solutions to optimize care (Kesselheim, Cresswell et al., 2011). Consumers, not just patients, are more participatory than ever before in managing their health; health care will no longer be confined to physicians' offices and hospitals. Preventive strategies and wellness promotion will be an integral part of health care—a transition toward continuous care from episodic care, and an expansion of horizon from points of care to points of *life*. In late 2016, Kaiser Permanente of Northern California reported that it interacted more with patients virtually (e-mail, video, and telephone) than in-person, underscoring the growing importance of telehealth technologies in health care delivery (Tuckson, Edmunds et al., 2017). Finally, given growing security threats and the sensitivity of personalized data, health care systems will be accountable for their protective role of patient privacy and security in health data transmission and storage. All these opportunities and challenges on the horizon require health care leaders to ensure their technology infrastructure can progressively become more interoperable, secure, and adaptable to new advances.

A SHARED VISION

Looking ahead, the most compelling aspiration of accelerating an interoperable health IT infrastructure is to support a person-centric, high-value, and continuously learning health system. In an ideal state, the person—and all of the surrounding systems and devices—are "known" entities and can integrate and share information seamlessly and for mutual benefit. As an individual enters or leaves a health system, information associated with each episode of care becomes a part of his or her longitudinal record for continued use both within and outside of the health delivery system. The medical record of the future is continuous, dynamic, and mobile and has built-in attributes that make an individual known, understood, and cared for with greater wisdom and precision.

Interoperable clinical and nonclinical data, coupled with analytic tools to filter signals from noise, will be foundational for any care delivery system that thrives for delivering timely, coordinated, outcome-focused, and patient-centered care. Data exchanges are extensive and speedy, mediated through trusted and secure mechanisms. Health care systems can acquire new health IT software or hardware components to enhance care quality or fill service gaps from multiple vendors that offer compatible modules with clear performance and price specifications. Established corporations and entrepreneurial businesses alike can bring innovative IT products to market with enhanced capabilities and uses that work seamlessly with existing architecture. Patients and consumers can access their own health information, determine which parties are granted access to their data, and actively participate in their own health and health care regardless of their demographic background, financial means, geographic location, and technology savviness.

ACTION AGENDA

A person-centric model allows patients, providers, vendors, and regulators to collaborate in an informed and synchronistic way that will significantly improve the safety of health care delivery, but it cannot be created without the cooperation, support and initiative of the entire health care community. Despite some promising pilot efforts, the health care sector is still substantially distant from integrating technology and sharing data across care settings in a way that will inform providers and patients in making smarter and safer decisions at the point of care. Health care applications in particular will need more efficient ways to combine and convert data from multiple sources, including automating conversion from unstructured to structured data (Raghupathi and Raghupathi, 2014). In the health IT marketplace, a collective move toward open architecture and an open business model will increasingly remove barriers of adopting new applications and devices, which will enable organizations to make nimble technology investments to support an overall trend toward shared risk management and accountability.

Despite the multipronged advances in promoting interoperability, the field is in a very early phase in terms of converging on a common approach to be adopted widely. The difficulty with regard to health care technology is that advances have been so rapid, and solutions have been so complex, that the "natural" evolution toward standardization faces many barriers. If progress is to be made anytime soon, it will require significant demand from users, to use marketing terminology, rather than waiting for a push from suppliers. This is particularly true at the point of care. Rather than continuing to be constrained by the high-cost proprietary status quo, in an ideal state, health systems would work with payers and device manufacturers to demand and adopt a platform that is standards based, addresses one-to-many communication, allows two-way data exchange in real time, and enables comprehensive integration of devices and systems. Standards development must include the creation of clinical use cases with conformance test tools that measure the quality of the standards and show they meet the needs of relevant use cases and workflows.

ROLES OF HEALTH CARE PROVIDER ORGANIZATIONS

Many health care organizations recognize the potential benefits—including improving care, increasing operational efficiency, and lowering costs—that are achievable through the seamless exchange of information and technology integration. However, it will always be a balancing act and leadership dilemma in pursuit of better technology and other competing priorities and resource constraints. Further, innovation accelerates at such a pace that a single health delivery system cannot confront the complex and costly tasks of data and technology integration on its own. At its root, the lack of interoperability is not merely a technical problem but is also a business-interest problem, and it is a fundamental problem on social and moral grounds. As the organizations buying, implementing, and using technologies to care for patients, health care providers can and must transform the technological underpinnings of the health care industry. Purchasers can reward vendors and developers that work together to adhere to the agreed-upon blueprint, thereby instilling confidence that solutions will work as expected, safely and securely (Cantwell and McDermott, 2016) as well as partner to create sufficient incentives to drive transformative change in the marketplace.

For health care organizations increasingly called upon to serve as population health stewards, lack of data liquidity and interoperability also impedes effective collaboration with community partners in providing effective and efficient whole-person care. At the macro-tier, data hoarding and data blocking remain common practice—which requires a combination of regulatory disincentives and, more importantly, a cultural shift. The 21st Century Cures Act's provision for civil penalties on information blocking serves as one exemplary policy lever, but a substantive cultural shift will require a concerted effort from many stakeholders. Health care providers, group purchasing organizations, payers, and other end users of health data must work together to accelerate bidirectional exchange of clinical, claims, care management, and psychosocial data that enables the ability to stratify patients according to risk, close gaps of care, and drive the development of a longitudinal patient record embedded in provider workflows.

Health care organizations and their service providers must also increase their investment in information risk management to protect against privacy breaches and cyberattacks. New threat agents such as state-sponsored hackers and ransomware, coupled with new vulnerabilities such as insufficiently protected devices and unpatched applications, have increased the ease and the rewards of stealing health information.

As market navigators and knowledge brokers, group purchasing organizations (GPOs) may also play a role in ushering collective purchasing power to send a clear signal to the marketplace (United States Government Accountability Office, 2010). With approximately 72 percent of hospital purchases contracted through GPOs, these organizations command sizable buying influence (Dobson DaVanzo & Associates, 2014). GPOs and similar advisory entities should provide technical contracting support to ensure their buyers' demands for connectivity are met with requiring the best-in-class standards, which are specified in the RFPs in detail. Doing what they do best, GPOs may then help achieve affordable solutions as health care systems continuously enhance interoperability and security of their health IT infrastructure.

The unified voice of the leaders of health care provider organizations consistently demanding interoperability from vendors would benefit purchasers and sellers alike, because the need to create and support custom solutions imposes a financial burden on vendors. For vendors, a centralized approach that specifies common requirements in RFPs and contracts could provide a focal point for engaging customers in solving shared technical challenges and could make enlisting the help of other industries easier. Breaking legacy paradigms is one of the most challenging, yet most critical, aspects of revamping data flow in health care. Learning from other industries that have conquered similar challenges is important, particularly how wide adoption of an open architecture business model eventually spurs innovations, resulting in more product choices and lower costs. Appendix A, Section 4 describes two case studies from the defense industry.

ROLES FOR THE FEDERAL GOVERNMENT

As a payer, provider, and regulator of health care, the federal government asserts substantial influence over the speed of health IT interoperability. In addition to various steps taken to incentivize greater interoperability as directed by the ONC Interoperability Roadmap, the federal government can also provide a platform for fostering macro-, meso-, and micro-tier interoperability while ensuring privacy and security. For example, it can help improve requirements specification through standards, develop methods and procedures to test systems against these standards, provide a testing infrastructure, help communities in building test tools, establish a clearinghouse to curate and catalogue software systems and point-of-care devices, and ensure that appropriate methodologies are available to various stakeholders for achieving interoperability. The federal government should also continue to publish test results (on websites such as the ONC Certified Health IT Product List and Office of the National Coordinator for Health Information Technology) of the different vendor systems to facilitate an open market for components that are interoperable for integration into customized architectures. Moreover, federal agencies should develop a consistent framework to incorporate interoperability in its IT product certification programs or criteria of approval for certain medical devices. As new privacy and security threats quickly evolve, regulatory agencies also need to respond with new rulings and guidance. For example, the Food and Drug Administration (FDA) issued guidelines for medical device manufacturers and health care facilities to take steps in ensuring that medical equipment does not become a vector for cyberattacks.

The 21st Century Cures Act provides several opportunities to spark further advances in health IT interoperability. This includes the establishment of penalties for information blocking ($1 million per occurrence), which could play a role in macro-tier data exchanges. ONC's enforcement of the Act by activating the Trusted Exchange Framework and Common Agreement (TEFCA) can be a strong vehicle to drive adoption of interoperability. As of March 2018, the ONC had received more than 200 public comments on the proposed draft TEFCA, including from the Health Information Technology Advisory Committee. Three potential outcomes are expected from the final configuration of TEFCA. First, patients can access their health information electronically without any special

effort. Second, providers and other accountable organizations can receive necessary and appropriate information about a group of individuals without having
to access one record at a time. This allows them to analyze population health
outcomes, identify at-risk populations, and track progress on quality improvement initiatives. Third, the health IT community can have open and accessible
APIs to encourage entrepreneurial, user-focused innovation to make health
information more accessible and EHRs more usable. By the end of 2018, a
recognized coordinating entity will be selected that uses TEFCA's policies, procedures, technical standards, principles, and goals to develop a single Common
Agreement that Qualified Health Information Networks and their participants
can voluntarily adopt.

The federal government can also provide incentives for providers and vendors
to enhance interoperability, including but not limited to adopting recommended
standards, as well as disincentives for information blocking. With a synergistic
goal of empowering patients through access to their health care data, in March
2018 the White House Office of American Innovation and the Centers for
Medicare and Medicaid Services (CMS) launched the MyHealthEData initiative. The initiative aims to break down barriers that prevent patients from
having electronic access and control over their own health records from the
device or application of their choice. One example is the Blue Button 2.0 API,
which leverages the FHIR standard to enable Medicare beneficiaries to share
their claims data with third-party application developers. The CMS also
announced the intention to overhaul its EHR Incentive Programs—now referred
to as the Procuring Interoperability program—to streamline the Meaningful
Use and the Quality Payment Program and intensify focus on interoperability,
preventing information blocking, and reducing reporting burden. Ongoing
considerations in expanding technology certifications beyond EHRs and in
providing clarity on the consequences of using noncertified technologies can
further drive market incentives. These laudable plans, if followed by rules and
programs reflecting careful considerations of stakeholder inputs and backed with
sufficient resources, can fuel a movement toward patient-centered interoperability
for the field.

Finally, as a major provider of health care and purchaser of health care IT
products, federal agencies should continue to share their procurement practices,
vendor lists, and interoperability requirement specifications with the public. As
pioneers in adopting a standards-based process for procurement of interoperable and secure health technology, the Departments of Defense and of Veterans
Affairs represent strong buying power and knowledge hubs. When working in
concert with other health care providers and payers, the health IT marketplace

BOX 2

Veterans Affairs' Procurement Principles to Support Veteran Care and National Interoperability

As the largest health system in the country, the Department of Veterans Affairs (VA) manages nine million veteran beneficiaries across 1,243 health care facilities, including 170 VA Medical Centers and 1,063 outpatient facilities. The Veterans Health Administration, the health care arm of the VA, also partners with approximately 450,000 community network providers (e.g., contracted network medical facilities, group practices, academic medical centers, and individual providers) who deliver more than 30 percent of our care to eligible veterans. High community network utilization by the veterans drives the VA to adopt models for integrated health care delivery. Building on federally incentivized adoption of certified EHR among community providers through programs such as the Medicare and Medicaid EHR Incentive Program, in 2017 the VA developed an Electronic Health Record Modernization plan that includes transitioning from legacy solutions to a commercial EHR solution.

To support current and future needs, the VA has developed the following interim procurement-focused principles:

- **Create integrated systems of care:** To empower our veterans and provide them with more choices, we must provide secure access to valuable medical information across the VA, DoD, academic medical centers, and private community provider facilities through standardized, commercial best practice transaction mechanisms.

- **Build intelligent networks:** To improve value, the VA is integrating standardized, evidence-based protocols at the points of care through the promotion and procurement of integrated and interoperable medical devices to aid in medical decision making and improve patient safety.

- **Establish an adaptable platform and adopt common standards:** The VA is creating an open API management platform to promote better, faster exchange of medical, benefits, human resource, and financial data. This will not only enhance veterans' care but also advance knowledge sharing, clinical decision support, medical device interoperability, technical expertise, and process interoperability. Solutions procured by the VA will use leading data and informatics industry standards (e.g., FHIR, LOINC, and others). Further, by shifting technology development to commercial developers through the expansion of the Lighthouse Lab, a software platform offering access tools for mobile and web application developers, it allows modular technology integration into the VA's enterprise system to provide holistic service to our veterans and encourage industry adoption and innovation. The VA is encouraging providers to join the Open API Pledge, to accelerate the mapping of health data to industry standards.

- **Foster transformational innovation:** As the market evolves, it is crucial that the VA meets the demands of current users while adopting innovations that further enable patient engagement through their preferred mode of communication and care (i.e., telehealth, connected medical devices). Through future contracts, the VA will promote innovation by extending APIs, enabling commercial developers to integrate directly with VA EHRs using SMART on FHIR (also see Box A1-3) and other integration approaches. By liberating data and enhancing interoperability, the VA aims to shift ownership of the data to the veterans and make data more readily available to patients and their caregivers.

Looking forward, the VA is focused on four areas of interoperability:

- VA Enterprise: The VA has notably achieved enterprise-wide interoperability through their long-standing legacy systems, but the aging technology significantly constrained interoperability. As we modernize our EHR system through the procurement of commercial off-the-shelf (COTS) product, we improve intra-VA interoperability by leveraging new and emerging technologies that more easily adapt and integrate with leading standards to support veteran access to information through preferred channels, including mobile devices.
- VA-DoD: As soldiers, sailors, and airmen transition from active duty and reserve to veteran status, maintaining quality and continuity of care are essential. The VA is working toward a seamless integration in this arena, as the VA procured the same EHR system as the DoD.
- Community Care: The VA is focused on further connecting with community providers beyond care summaries, by sharing pertinent encounter and medical data, along with seamless appointment scheduling, authorization, and reimbursements. Lessons learned and population health information will be used with near-real-time Clinical Decision Support technologies to ensure that we are providing the best care possible.
- National Interoperability: With a large community provider network and deep partnerships with the academic medical community, the VA is uniquely positioned to act as a catalyst for national interoperability. Collaborating with commercial market experts, the VA aims to accelerate interoperability across the industry through adoption of best practices and emerging technologies (i.e., open API platform, artificial intelligence, robotics, and blockchain). Data security remains paramount, and veterans must continue to trust that their data is handled with advanced cybersecurity protocols.

SOURCE: Ashwini Zenooz, US Department of Veterans Affairs

can be propelled in a new direction. Referenced previously, *Box 1* described initiatives at the Department of Defense. A related initiative of central importance is underway at the Department of Veterans Affairs; *Box 2* details ongoing health IT procurement strategies, aiming to continuously improve veteran care and support interoperability nationwide.

ROLES FOR PAYERS

Although the majority of this assessment focuses on health care providers who acquire health IT products through procurement, payers also play a pivotal role in shaping the marketplace incentives and norms. Both public and commercial payers have many levers that can significantly shift the interoperability goals and value proposition for health care organizations. Moreover, payment contracts and reporting requirements can set the expectation for data sharing, security, and compliance to standards.

Payers have several motivations to foster digital interoperability through procurement: first and foremost is care quality and value improvement. When clinical and administrative data can flow more effortlessly, governmental and commercial payers can benefit from the reduced cost and redundancy of services, lower rates of patient harm, and greater ability to monitor care quality and outcomes. This may extend beyond the three tiers of interoperability discussed earlier to include telemedicine and beyond. One study by Fallon Health reported a savings of $687 per member per month by adopting a remote monitoring system that allows seniors to safely live in their homes longer while reducing cost of care (Healthsense, 2016).

Secondly, payers currently incur substantial operating costs from maintaining data exchange interfaces with a network of providers that are exchanging data through various record management systems, data formats, and interfaces. A movement toward a common data exchange platform that allows modular add-ons for predictive analytic tools to process multiple streams of data feeds can eliminate the costs of technology integration for many payers.

A third motivation is the pursuit of population health and continuous learning. With the increase in the number of patients with multiple chronic conditions and complex needs, payers should actively partner with providers to advance care delivery and promote health and wellness of high-needs patients. To generate actionable insight, payers need a trusted data exchange framework to securely obtain interoperable clinical and claims data, as well as the ability to add predictive analytic tools on the back end for population health management.

Some commercial and governmental payers already assert influence with regard to health care data interoperability. For example, contractual agreements may include requirement for data sharing, file format and field definitions, privacy and security, and the reporting time frame. Payers can collectively agree on specific interoperability standards and provide specific technical guidance for providers to use in their procurement specifications. Moreover, payers can strategically embed incentives for adopting certified technology capable of sharing information, essentially lowering the cost of adoption for providers with more constrained resources. Payers are also positioned to send a clear signal that elevates the priority to make socio-demographic, behavioral, and other personal data interoperable—so that the care is optimized for "point of life" and not just point of care. Another approach is to explicitly provide incentives for the use of wearable, mobile technology, and telemedicine modules that include remote monitoring. Such information traditionally resides outside of care settings, and there are substantial technical and cultural barriers to integrating them.

Finally, public and commercial payers should actively engage in the formation of a health IT procurement "commons." They should participate in building shared, national resources for procurement specifications, interoperability and data-sharing quality measurement, testing and certification of plug-and-play technologies, and the recognition of common standards and architecture.

ROLES FOR HEALTH IT VENDORS

Industry leaders often highlight the fact that, although technology to enable interoperability generally exists, until the recent past, market forces have not created sufficient incentives to offer interoperability as a key feature. Even with increasingly aligned market incentives, some companies still view the adoption of open interfaces as detrimental to their current competitive advantage—selling bundled solutions or a system of devices with closed, proprietary interfaces. On the other hand, policy and regulatory mechanisms have been progressively driving vendors to demonstrate, if not compete on, interoperability. This has been the case for the macro-tier under various federal requirements and incentive programs, where providers and EHR vendors have to demonstrate data exchange capabilities with other health care institutions, HIEs, and government agencies. Market forces have also begun to shift focus to value-based payment models that prioritize interoperability at higher levels than what was true in pure fee-for-service settings.

Another major driver of change is the pressing need to mitigate risk exposure associated with cyberbreaches and unsecured technologies. In 2012, the "Internet of things" was barely on the radar, but today Internet-connected medical infrastructure and medical devices have to be top of mind for security teams.

For medical systems and devices at large, achieving extended, modular connectivity will often require the development of new interfaces or adapters, for which both device makers and providers bear the costs. The collaborative development of an open architecture platform that uses a small number of agreed-upon data exchange standards will require active participation of IT vendors. As seen in other industries, such alignment with other stakeholders is the only way to ensure that health care providers and the system and device manufacturers can both reap the benefit of increased interoperability and adoption of common standards. The transition away from closed, proprietary interfaces may require a shift in tactics in competing for market share in the device industry, but it may prove to diversify product risks and shorten the time from innovation to delivery in settings where good standards exist.

Software platform and application vendors should demonstrate how data captured from external sources can be integrated into clinical workflows, and the value of such integration. Only when these use cases are adequately evaluated and their value widely replicated in multiple settings will providers demand interoperability and open solutions and reward vendors who embrace open-architecture principles.

As EHR systems remain a hub for aggregating the patient care experience and treatment progress, EHR vendors will exert a key influence in the market dynamics and expectations. Health IT system vendors should work together to agree upon the best industry standard exchange specifications and then make them available to their customers. Two recent examples are the CommonWell Health Alliance and Carequality, multivendor collaborations to improve document sharing among the members. Recently, CommonWell and Carequality have agreed to interconnect their networks, furthering the reach of document exchange.

Finally, vendors of patient-connected technologies such as telemedicine modules and wearable technologies should actively engage patients and families in their technology development and improvement while developing a vigorous security and privacy protection framework that respects their data exchange wishes. Established platforms should also contribute to a shared testing infrastructure for device manufacturers and mobile technology innovators to test connectivity with enterprise systems.

V.

PERSPECTIVES ON THE ISSUE: AN NAM PUBLIC SYMPOSIUM

In addition to consultations and literature reviews to elicit perspectives and experiences from the field, the National Academy of Medicine convened a daylong listening and discussion meeting among health care delivery system leaders and related stakeholders. The purpose of the meeting was to critically review the current state of interoperability, evaluate the recommendations discussed in the earlier draft of this report, and discuss barriers to and priorities for establishing true digital integration across the nation's health care system. Participants and attendees included representatives of government agencies, health care systems, health IT companies, and other organizations concerned with health care delivery or advocacy. Through this dialogue, health care delivery system leaders explored ways to partner with each other in charting the glide path toward mission- and value-driven health technology acquisition. Meeting participants highlighted the fact that procurement is only one of many factors at play; regulations, incentives, and other market forces have to converge to truly move the needle. Meeting participants also stressed the need to accelerate interoperability to power consumer- and patient-centered care delivery in a cost-effective and equitable fashion. Feedback received from the discussion has been used in producing the final version of this Special Publication. The full agenda and the list of participants are in Appendix B, and the session recordings are available online at https://nam.edu/interoperability.

MEETING SUMMARY

After opening remarks by Victor Dzau and Michael McGinnis from the National Academy of Medicine and Harvey Fineberg of the Moore Foundation, David J. Shulkin, Secretary of Veterans Affairs (VA), offered his support for the goal, underscoring that the VA is looking at how its own procurement policies can be a model and facilitator of a nationwide solution to interoperability.

> *This conference is coming at a very good time for what we are dealing with at the VA . . . We are looking now at how we, with the largest implementation of electronic medical records in the history of the country, can help drive [national interoperability] . . . We want to be part of the ideas and solutions that you are creating today. We think this is absolutely essential that we get this right, not only for the VA but for the country, and we believe that now is the right time to do this.*
>
> — DAVID J. SHULKIN, *US Secretary of Veterans Affairs*

Three stage-setting panels in the morning focused on the current landscape for interoperability in health care, the content and recommendations of the draft paper, and system-wide strategic considerations for interoperability. The afternoon panels assessed marketplace contributions, strategic priorities for health care system leaders, and CEO perspectives on the topic. The day ended with a discussion of priority steps. Presented here are representative key points from the day's presentations and discussions.

OVERVIEW OF INTEROPERABILITY IN HEALTH CARE

In setting the stage for the day's discussions, the first panel reviewed definitions and core elements of interoperability; the current status of digital interoperability in health, including roles and the status of existing standards; previous and ongoing initiatives to promote interoperability; and barriers and rate-limiting factors.

Don Rucker, Office of the National Coordinator for Health IT, pointed out that health IT has made great progress in the last decade, moving from almost entirely paper-based medical records to a penetration of 86 percent among office-based physicians and 98 percent among hospitals and health systems (Office of the National Coordinator for Health Information Technology). In addition, 93 percent of hospitals offer patients online access to health information through a portal. Four out of five hospitals allow patients to download their health information, reported Chantal Worzala of American Hospital Association, and a growing number of hospitals offer online prescription refill requests, appointment scheduling, bill payment, and secure messaging with providers (American Hospital Association [AHA], 2018). Much of the progress can be attributed to the regulations and incentives included in the HITECH Act and other government programs, but consumer demand and cost efficiency have also played a role.

Part of the reason why the prevalence of EHRs—and the increasing amount of data within organizations—has not translated into significantly improved clinical decision making or health outcomes is related to the limited capacity for seamless cross-communication and information exchange. Multiple EHR platforms and versions of platforms complicate the sharing of health information across and even within health organizations. Regional Health Information Exchanges have had only limited success on a local level, but even less on a national level. The development of standards such as open APIs, RESTful, JSON, and especially FHIR has helped in some instances, but has not solved the problem. At this point, most interactions involve pushing data—sending a patient's record or aggregate data from one health care entity to another. Some organizations are starting to pull data (query and retrieve), but this has proved to be much more difficult. At points of care, data do not flow easily among the many devices used in patient care both in hospitals and in outpatient settings. Interoperability becomes a potential patient safety and efficiency concern when devices at a patient's bedside cannot talk to each other or to the EHR.

The issue has garnered the attention of Congress, said Rucker. The 21st Century Cures Act passed in 2015 contains language on interoperability to encourage open APIs "without special effort" and establishes penalties for information blocking (114th Congress, 2015).

The demand for interoperability has grown with new models of care that require more granular data sharing and data sharing both within and beyond the health care system. Value-based reimbursement depends on access to outcomes data and improving population health requires information sharing with organizations that address the social determinants of health. Several panelists pointed out that the definition of interoperability may need to be broadened to center less on providers and the health system, and more on making information usable and useful at both the level of the individual patient and at the population level. Although health information sharing had increased each year, significant barriers remain, including cumbersome workflow of information sharing, difficulties identifying the correct patient, increased challenges when exchanging information across different vendors' platforms, and recipients reporting that information is not useful.

Of primary importance to interoperability initiatives is ensuring data security throughout the process. This has been, and remains, a core patient interest, perhaps impeding demand for interoperability. But that may be changing. Although the level of consumer demand and expectation for interoperability has not been as great as in banking and other industries, fluid data exchange is necessary to benefit patient and population health. More and more, patients and families express frustrations at its failures.

Part of the reason we are having problems with interoperability is that we have defined it too narrowly—in a very provider-centric way for a very long time. Historically, it has been from Provider A to Provider B about one patient . . . We need to think about interoperability in a much broader way, not as a onesies game but on a population level.

— DON RUCKER, *Office of the National Coordinator for Health IT,*
US Department of Health and Human Services

Interoperability is one of the most complex things we are trying to undertake in health care today . . . First, we need to make sure the right regulations and incentives are there . . . We then need to have the structure and technical capability to move information. Even if you were to get the information where it needs to go, the processes need to be in place so people needing to see the information can see it to make a decision. Last but not least, we need to make sure that information is needed, trusted, and accurate to be incorporated into a clinical decision. Each of these levels from the broader environment down to the individual decision makers is all dependent on each other. We've made tremendous progress, but we're trying to do something that's really hard.

— JULIE ADLER-MILSTEIN, *University of California, San Francisco*

Also considered in the conversation was the issue of needed regulatory actions, clearly necessary for standards but not without consequences. For example, Chantal Worzala of the American Hospital Association reported that nonclinical aspects of regulations cost the hospital industry $39 billion per year, or about $7.6 million per hospital or $1,200 per patient. Health IT ranks third in terms of this regulatory burden, behind billing and coding (American Hospital Association [AHA] 2018). So, interoperability's ability to reduce that burden is an important point needing elaboration.

NAM SPECIAL PUBLICATION ON PROCURING INTEROPERABILITY

Peter Pronovost, co-chair of the project's steering committee, presented the special publication in its draft form, which focused on leveraging procurement to foster interoperability across macro-, meso-, and micro-tiers. Working along with other forces at play, the vision is to provide consumers a seamless experience that also reduces burden of care on providers, increases patient safety, decreases the number of medical errors, and reduces costs. The five action steps health care administrators can take to ensure interoperability—commit, identify, collaborate, specify, and assess—were presented to the audience, as well as the Technical Supplement, which laid out the framework for using the procurement process to advance interoperability at the institutional, regional, and national level, and included sample RFP language.

The steering committee drew lessons learned from other industries, such as cable television and the military, on how they moved from disparate systems to a more standard-based, modular purchasing model that allowed different segments to communicate more easily. One missing piece in health care is for purchasers of technology to specify their demand for interoperability in clear, technical terms within their purchase agreements and RFPs. By specifying interoperability requirements for new equipment and systems, health care administrators can collectively propel vendors to align around data exchange standards and to design interoperability into their products. The goal of this process is data liquidity, the free exchange of useful data for the benefit of all involved, in particular to patients and families who must be both cocreators and prime beneficiaries of the work.

The caregivers at point of care, the people delivering the health care infrastructure, and the people who are receiving health care have to be involved in the design process. We do not need to make the mistake that we made so many times in developing our systems, whether it is reimbursement systems or IT systems. We need the insights of the subject matter experts—in this case, the clinicians and caregivers at the point of care.

— MEREDITH KARNEY, *Center for Medical Interoperability*

Panelists from different perspectives offered the business case for making the investment in interoperability, and their thoughts on the recommendations. They pointed out that, in other industries, a perceived crisis pushed leaders into action. Yet such a burning platform has not taken place in US health care despite the fact that nearly 20 percent of GDP spending is in health care while the United States shows poorer outcomes than other developed countries (Council and Population, 2013). Patient safety concerns should also push progress in interoperability. It is time, said Ashwini Zenooz, the VA's chief medical officer of EHR modernization, to all play together on the same field for the sake of patients, effectiveness, and efficiency of care.

SYSTEM-WIDE STRATEGIC CONSIDERATIONS

Interoperability, by its very nature, has wide-ranging implications for all sectors and stakeholders in the health care system. It affects patient safety, patient access to data, provider burnout, and cost of care. In the third panel of the day, health care leaders reflected on some of the system-wide strategic considerations in formulating approaches to interoperability. Several themes emerged:

Patient safety is the key motivator

Today's health care environment requires integrated technologies and rich data to prevent patient harm, enable learning, and transform care delivery models, said Julian Goldman from Partners Healthcare. In an era with new technologies and gadgets generating new data streams every day, health system leaders and administrators should prioritize and plan for interoperability to make our clinical environments safer and less prone to human error, but also to, first and foremost, set the stage for transformational progress in health care performance.

Technology should alleviate, not add to clinician burden

Clinician burnout and dissatisfaction is a critical issue for health care and one contributing factor to the clinician shortage in some parts of the country. One of the leading "dissatisfiers" for physicians is EHRs, reported Laura McGraw of the American Medical Association. She stressed that interoperability solutions should reduce—not increase—the burden on physicians, yet the current state of practice falls far short in that respect. In addition to patient safety concerns, the lack of smart cross-checking among devices at the bedside leads to alarm fatigue among clinicians. When clinicians choose what to record from a patient monitoring device in the EHR, a single number may not adequately reflect what is happening to the patient, said Andy Gettinger of the Office of the National Coordinator for Health IT.

Data liquidity is not merely a technology problem

The goal is to make the right information available at the right time and place to improve clinical decision making—which requires data liquidity. Ed Miller from the Center for Medical Interoperability pointed out that this isn't a technology problem; the capabilities exist. The key, he said, is aligning an ecosystem for facile information sharing.

Cybersecurity and trust affect pace of progress

Security breaches and hacking incidents within and outside of health care in recent years have caused great fear that accelerating data exchange may leave systems vulnerable to cyberattacks. However, the experience in other industries shows that interoperability does not have to compromise security. While demanding clear cybersecurity functionalities in procurement matters, the industry needs to develop and adopt secure data exchange protocols and identity management practices. Contrary to one belief, a participant posited, in many cases data exchanges using open APIs can actually be safer than locking systems down into separate silos.

ACCELERATING MARKETPLACE CONTRIBUTIONS TO INTEROPERABILITY

Access to data is an important part of a learning health system that is continuously moving toward the triple aim of better health, better care, and lower cost—or the "quadruple aim" that also factors in the importance of individual engagement. The different players in the health care ecosystem—including health care providers, software and device manufacturers, payers, and data engineers—can all contribute to hastening the pace of change and pushing the system closer to true interoperability. Representatives from several companies spoke on this topic during a lunchtime panel, sharing their concerns and ideas on how best to move toward interoperability.

Chuck Martel from Anthem, Inc. diagnosed health care with "clinical data disorder," a disease for which the treatment plan is still in development. "Data [represents] the health care system's most valuable and, to date, underutilized asset," he said. Simply digitizing the disorder of paper records is not enough to harness the capabilities of technologies; information must flow in order to be effective for the common good. In collaboration with seven hospital systems and using the FHIR resources, Anthem has established a private health information exchange that allows for aggregating administrative and clinical data into a holistic, longitudinal patient record.

Bram Stolk introduced his company, GE Healthcare, as a manufacturer of "devices that create the data that we're trying to make interoperable." Vendors must come together to start to create a uniform structure—and then not dilute the utility of data by adding proprietary fields. He added that companies like his must sell their products to make a profit, and profits drive action. Echoing the report's call for enhancing procurement specifications, "the only way for vendors to conform is when it's in the purchasing agreement," he said.

David McCallie from Cerner pointed out that reimbursement drives the structure of EHRs. Clinicians cannot enter free notes, because everything needs to be coded for reimbursement. This limits the usefulness of the record for other purposes. Value-based reimbursement—and the emphasis on population health, personalized medicine, and addressing the social determinants of health—reinforces the need for interoperability and widens the network beyond the traditional health care system. Information exchange needs to be incorporated into the workflow so that it can be used for wellness, diagnosis, insights, and decision making, added Rob Klootwyk from Epic. "It's time to move from viewing to doing more with data," said Klootwyk, "for the good of patients and to promote population health."

Google is focusing on interoperability from a population health perspective, Eyal Oren explained. He pointed out that data harmonization—the process by which institutions aggregate and structure data to suit reporting and other purposes—can make raw data less available to machine learning, deep learning, and other emerging large-scale analytic approaches.

> *We have technologies that are able to amass tremendous insights, recommendations, and learnings from data, but how and whether they will actually transform reality for people depends on the fundamental driver, which is always money. We have a lot of technologies that will increase quality, but how and when it actually impacts reality remains to be seen. It all depends on the ecosystem, the reimbursement models, and providers and payers.*
>
> — EYAL OREN, *Google*

STRATEGIC PRIORITIES FOR HEALTH CARE SYSTEM LEADERS

The afternoon started with a discussion among health system leaders on "where they sit and what they see" as they pursue interoperability within their organizations.

Admiral Raquel Bono, director of the Defense Health Agency (DHA), which administers 55 hospitals and 350 clinics in the United States and overseas, talked about how her agency wants to become a market force for interoperability as it works to create a value-based, integrated system of readiness and health. To give a glimpse of the challenge, she explained that 30,000 different types of intravenous (IV) pumps are in use in the DHA system and as many as 4,000 in the Pacific Northwest alone. Only three of these met standards for interoperability and cybersecurity. Having standard, interoperable, and secure equipment helps ensure that the person using the equipment on the battlefield has the requisite training to use it safely, she noted.

As chief health information officer of a large for-profit health system, Jim Jirjis of HCA Healthcare said his goal is to make it easy for patients to get care and affiliate physicians to give care at HCA's 175 hospitals. He would like to use the vast amount of data captured at HCA's facilities to ensure the quality of care and value for patients and payers and to improve the work environment for the system's 70,000 nurses and other clinicians. Interoperability is a necessary ingredient for making this happen, he said. However, he thought that procurement alone would not be enough to achieve the goal. He also supported both policy and financial incentives for vendors to work together toward common interoperability standards and platform.

> We're at a crossroads with our company and in health care. Our leadership are awakening to the power of our clinical data. Health care is a highly information-intensive industry; information has to flow . . . There is a real opportunity to use that for real time, just-in-time patient care . . . We are not unique in these subchallenges. I think there will be tremendous alignment with other providers, organizations, and systems that are entrusted with the delivery of highly regulated care.
>
> — JIM JIRJIS, *HCA Healthcare*

As Chip Kahn of the Federation of American Hospitals pointed out, the lesson from HITECH is that money and regulation drive action. Although Admiral Bono "didn't disagree" with the need for regulatory guidance on interoperability, she thought that collectively the health care industry could drive and shape the market without relying on regulation.

HEALTH CARE C-SUITE PERSPECTIVES

Continuing the discussion from the C-suite perspective, the last panel of the day featured CEOs and CIOs from Mayo Clinic, Johns Hopkins Medicine, Cleveland Clinic, Montefiore Medicine, and Community Care Network of Virginia. They shared their experiences and perspectives on interoperability and its role in health care improvement.

Stephanie Reel, CIO at Johns Hopkins Medicine, pointed to her institution's emphasis on patient safety. Without interoperability, it is difficult to get a precise view of what is happening with patients and to deliver effective and efficient care, she said. She thought that to capture the attention of health care CEOs, interoperability must be framed in terms of controlling cost, expanding coverage, improving the patient experience, and—most importantly—delivering safe, effective, and efficient care.

Other considerations that drive the quest for interoperability include the financial pressures on health care. Toby Cosgrove of Cleveland Clinic said the ability to deal with data can help drive efficiencies that can bring costs down. Several panelists and audience members pointed out that upgrading and switching out health IT systems—especially proprietary platforms—can be very costly both financially and in terms of labor. Interoperability has the potential to make the process of switching and upgrading health IT less burdensome.

The CEO of Montefiore Medicine, Steve Safyer, and the CEO of Community Care Network of Virginia, Rene Cabral-Daniels—both of whose organizations serve predominantly Medicaid populations—were excited about the potential to reach beyond the health care system to social service organizations through interoperability, noting that social determinants of health may affect patient outcomes more than health care. But such efforts add another layer of complexity. Cabral-Daniels recounted how Community Care of Virginia tried to share vaccination data with the Richmond school system. Even with willing partners, supportive funders, and adequate technological capabilities, sharing data across organizations and care settings proved difficult. The limited bandwidth at health care institutions may add to the challenge. Panelists agreed that market forces and regulation have to work in sync to drive action and bring about the alignment necessary to achieve interoperability.

SUMMARY SESSION

Reflecting the complexity of these issues, simple solutions were evasive, but several key next steps on the path to interoperability were posited. Attendees recognized that interoperability and data liquidity are a means to an end, rather than a goal by themselves. For purchasers of health information technologies, it is not merely a technical challenge at the organizational level, but a business process and a cultural challenge. However, there is tremendous potential in leveraging our individual and collective technology investment more purposefully toward better patient outcomes, increased health care value, and improved population health.

Health care delivery and its technology infrastructure are at a critical juncture today. Standards development and EHR adoption over the past decades lay a fertile ground for the next era of data liquidity, where key data across the care continuum—and across the life course—can trigger the right actions to the right person at the right time. In the marketplace, it is also a critical time to make sure that the type of competition among health care providers and among technology vendors is focused on quality and value, rather than on exclusivity and proprietorship of data.

Such movement in the acquisition of health IT requires concerted efforts from many stakeholders represented at the meeting, including health care providers, health IT vendors, societies and associations, standards organizations, federal agencies, and payers. There is a need for one or more neutral convening bodies that can coordinate the generation and dissemination of knowledge as well as practical solutions. More specifically, a testing and certification body is critical in representing a shared resource for health systems and technology innovators large and small to participate in the evolution.

Strategic procurement undoubtedly holds exciting potential to move the health system toward true interoperability, especially when combined with the right policy and market incentives. It takes strong leadership and negotiation among the different players. Using the engineering mind-set to start with the end in mind, health care leaders with different perspectives—such as information management, risk management, or financial—will have to collaborate to ensure they're working toward the same goals. Clinicians and patients must be part of the process, including those who are not part of large, well-resourced organizations, to achieve an equitable, people-centered learning health system.

VI.

PROCUREMENT IMPLEMENTATION: ACTION CHECKLIST

Seamless system-wide digital, structural, and functional interoperability is critically important for health and health care activities to meet their full potential and the fundamental aims for health care set out by the National Academy of Medicine (formerly the Institute of Medicine) in the 2000 report *Crossing the Quality Chasm*—care that is: safe, effective, patient-centered, timely, efficient, and equitable (Institute of Medicine, 2001). Rapidly-developing capacities of the digital infrastructure of health care bring us much closer to the potential for achieving that vision. Our clinicians and our administrative leaders must have access to meaningful information, delivered at the point of care and at the point of decision making, to promote excellence while ensuring affordability. Data liquidity and functional interoperability can help eliminate waste and reduce unwarranted variation in care—a prerequisite for optimally leveraging constrained resources. Seamless inter-provider and inter-facility communication can ensure continuous and well-connected care. Because current circumstances are far short of the potential, achieving the vision requires determined commitment and leadership throughout the health sector, beginning with the choices and requirements of those who directly interact with the patients and families whose care they are stewarding.

Requisite standards and policies are still evolving, and the process will be one of ongoing continuous improvement, but there are many ways to accelerate the progress. Presented next, in checklist form, are opportunities and responsibilities for those who lead health care delivery at the front line, and, to whom the performance of each item is entrusted by their patients and families.

HEALTH CARE ORGANIZATION BOARD AND EXECUTIVE TEAM

☐ **Understanding.** Has our organization explicitly and adequately assessed the experiences and potential consequences due to shortfalls in digital interoperability for patients, families, and clinicians?

☐ **Commitment.** Has our organization expressly committed to seamless and affordable interoperability and meaningful information sharing as a core element in the care we provide, and in every acquisition action for our systems, services, and tools? Have we devoted resources to initial investment, implementation, and training, as well as to ongoing needs for maintenance and continuous improvement?

☐ **Governance.** Have we established an organization-wide safety, security, and interoperability steering group accountable for driving progress and guiding organization-wide procurement activities?

☐ **Priorities.** Has our organization inventoried our interoperability shortfalls and established corrective priorities for those areas in which the care experience and outcomes are most vulnerable?

☐ **Procurements.** Is our organization participating in/drawing on best available sector-wide language for interoperability specification requirements in procurement agreements for all our systems, services, or tools?

☐ **Protocols.** Is our organization adhering to our procurement protocols and thresholds to implement system-wide functional digital interoperability as a requirement of our purchases?

☐ **Cooperation.** Is our organization fully cooperating with other health care systems, payers, associations, vendors, and standards agencies in supporting a shared capacity for system-wide digital interoperability testing, clinical use case assessment, and best-practice purchasing specifications and strategies?

☐ **Assessment.** Is our organization actively cooperating with other organizations on assessment approaches that measure and incentivize progress in digital interoperability in health and health care, and are we applying them to assessing the core continuity, connectivity, and safety experience of patients, families, and clinicians?

OTHER KEY STAKEHOLDERS

Achieving seamless and affordable system-wide digital interoperability will also require the vigorous commitment and leadership of other central stakeholders:

digital health technology vendors; employers and payers; associations and purchasing cooperatives; and federal government agencies. Corresponding action checklists are presented below.

Digital health technology vendors

☐ **Commitment.** Have we clearly committed to the promotion of sector-wide functional interoperability and connectivity as a core performance feature of our products and services?

☐ **Transparency.** Do we share with our clients the set of compatible data exchange interfaces and standards, as well as assess and share the interoperability performance of our products?

☐ **Cooperation.** Are we fully cooperating with health care systems, payers, associations, other vendors, and standards agencies in supporting a shared capacity for sector-wide digital interoperability testing, clinical use case assessment, and best-practice purchasing specifications and strategies?

Employers and payers

☐ **Commitment.** Have we expressly stated our commitment to full digital interoperability as a core feature in the care for which we pay?

☐ **Requirements.** Do we require the existence of an interoperability strategy, implementation plan, and milestones as a core feature of our contracts for care?

☐ **Patient access.** Have we embedded incentives in our purchasing standards to facilitate access to claims data by patients, families, and developers of patient-facing technologies?

☐ **Capacity incentives.** Have we embedded incentives in our purchasing standards for adopting technology with certified capacity for effective and efficient information storage and sharing, including socio-demographic and behavioral data relevant to population health management?

☐ **Data sharing.** Do we have operational data-sharing and all-payer claims strategies to improve access, efficiency, and transparency with our data exchange partners, including care coordination managers, clinicians, regulators, and patients?

☐ **Cooperation.** Are we fully cooperating with health care systems, other payers, associations, vendors, and standards agencies in supporting a shared capacity for sector-wide digital interoperability testing, clinical use case assessment, and best-practice interoperability purchasing specifications and strategies?

Associations and purchasing cooperatives

☐ **Commitment.** Have we expressly committed to full digital interoperability as a core feature of the purchases for which we are the fiduciaries?

☐ **Procurements.** Are we drawing on, and contributing to, sector-wide performance specification language for interoperability requirements in procurement agreements for systems, services, or tools?

☐ **Cooperation.** Are we fully cooperating with health care systems, payers, associations, vendors, and standards agencies in supporting a shared capacity for sector-wide digital interoperability testing, clinical use case assessment, and best-practice purchasing specifications and strategies for our members?

Federal government agencies

☐ **Commitment.** Have we expressly embedded seamless interoperability as a core expectation and priority for health policy, in the standards in which we invest, in the care we deliver, and in the care for which we pay?

☐ **Policies, standards, and regulations.** Are our policies, standards, and regulations carefully aligned to ensure the existence of both the foundational starting points for seamless digital interoperability and the strategic vehicles for practical adaptation and continuous improvement?

☐ **Facilitation.** Are we fully supporting, encouraging, and facilitating the cooperative work of health care systems, payers, associations, vendors, and standards agencies to develop a shared capacity for sector-wide digital interoperability testing, clinical use case assessment, and best-practice purchasing specifications and strategies?

☐ **Care delivery.** In each of our care delivery agencies, and for each of our care delivery facilities, have we established an organization-wide interoperability steering group to drive progress and guide organization-wide and system-wide procurement and implementation activities?

☐ **Care payment.** Do we require that each facility receiving our reimbursement for care have an active organization-wide interoperability steering group working intra- and inter-organizationally to drive progress?

☐ **Assessment.** Have we established the taxonomy of the features of system-wide interoperability, set in motion to assess progress and identify opportunities for continuous improvement within organizations and across the nation?

The emergence of digital technology as a resource for progress in health and health care will yield transformative progress. That potential is achievable, but will be captured only with the determination of all participants to take the necessary steps for seamless system-wide interoperability. The opportunities embedded in the checklists above represent initial steps on which to build and improve. The dividends for patients, families, and clinicians throughout the nation can be historic.

REFERENCES

114th Congress. 2015. 21st Century Cures Act, H.R. 34. Available from: https://www.congress.gov/114/plaws/publ255/PLAW-114publ255.pdf.

American Hospital Association (AHA). 2018. *Annual survey information technology supplement data brief*, March 2018.

Becker's Hospital CFO Report. 2011. *Average inpatient hospital stay shorter but more expensive in 2009 than 1997.* Available from: https://www.beckershospitalreview.com/finance/average-inpatient-hospital-stay-shorter-but-more-expensive-in-2009-than-1997.html.

Brigham, K. L., and M. M. E. Johns. 2012. *Predictive health: How we can reinvent medicine to extend our best years.* New York: Basic Books.

Cantwell, E., and K. McDermott. 2016. Making technology talk: How interoperability can improve care, drive efficiency, and reduce waste. Healthcare Financial Management Association, May. Available from: http://medicalinteroperability.org/wp-content/uploads/2016/04/Making-Technology-Talk_HFM-reprint_May2016.pdf.

Commission on Systemic Interoperability. 2005. Ending the document game: Connecting and transforming your healthcare through information technology. Available from: www.EndingTheDocumentGame.gov.

Dobson DaVanzo & Associates. 2014. A 2014 Update of Cost Savings and Marketplace Analysis of the Group Purchasing Industry. A report submitted to Healthcare Supply Chain Association (HSCA). Available from: https://c.ymcdn.com/sites/higpa.site-ym.com/resource/resmgr/research/hsca_cost_savings_group_purc.pdf

Fieler, V. K., T. Jaglowski, and K. Richards. 2013. Eliminating errors in vital signs documentation. *CIN: Computers, Informatics, Nursing* 31(9):422–427.

Flores, M., G. Glusman, K. Brogaard, N. D. Price, and L. Hood. 2013. P4 medicine: How systems medicine will transform the healthcare sector and society. *Personalized Medicine* 10(6):565–576.

Guertin, N., and T. Hurt. 2013. *DoD open systems architecture contract guidebook for program managers: A tool for effective competition.* Defense Acquisition University.

Healthsense. 2016. Remote monitoring system allows seniors to live in their homes longer AND reduces total medical expense by $687 per member per month. Available from: http://healthsense.com/about-healthsense/news-and-events/ press-releases/remote-monitoring-system-allows-seniors-to-live-in-their-homes-longer-and-reduces-total-medical-expense-by-687-per-member-per-month-3/.

Hendrich, A., M. P. Chow, B. A. Skierczynski, and Z. Lu. 2008. A 36-hospital time and motion study: How do medical-surgical nurses spend their time? *Permanente Journal* 12(3):25–34.

Holmgren, A. J., V. Patel, and J. Adler-Milstein. 2017. Progress in interoperability: Measuring US hospitals' engagement in sharing patient data. *Health Affairs (Millwood)* 36(10):1820–1827.

IEEE. 2016. Definition of interoperability. IEEE Standards University. Available from: https://www.standardsuniversity.org/article/standards-glossary/#I.

Institute of Medicine. 2001. *Crossing the quality chasm: A new health system for the 21st century.* Washington, DC: The National Academies Press.

Institute of Medicine. 2000. *To err is human: Building a safer health system.* Washington, DC: The National Academies Press.

JASON. 2013. A robust health data infrastructure. Available from: https://www. healthit.gov/sites/default/files/ptp13-700hhs_white.pdf.

JASON Report Task Force. 2014. JASON Report Task Force final report. Available from: https://www.healthit.gov/hitac/sites/faca/files/Joint_HIT_JTF%20 Final%20Report%20v2_2014-10-15.pdf.

Jha, A. K., D. C. Chan, A. B. Ridgway, C. Franz, and D. W. Bates. 2009. Improving safety and eliminating redundant tests: Cutting costs in U.S. hospitals. *Health Affairs (Millwood)* 28(5):1475–1484.

Kesselheim, A. S., K. Cresswell, S. Phansalkar, D. W. Bates, and A. Sheikh. 2011. Clinical decision support systems could be modified to reduce "alert fatigue" while still minimizing the risk of litigation. *Health Affairs* 30(12):2310–2317.

Lin, S. C., J. Everson, and J. Adler-Milstein. 2017. Technology, incentives, or both? Factors related to level of hospital health information exchange. Health Services Research.

Medical Device Plug-and-Play Interoperability & Cybersecurity (MD PnP) Program at Massachusetts General Hospital. 2018. MD FIRE (Medical Device Free Interoperability Requirements for the Enterprise) Contracting Language, V 2.6. http://mdpnp.mgh.harvard.edu/projects/md-fire/.

Moorman, B. 2010. *True costs of device connectivity.* Paper presented at the meeting of the Association for the Advancement of Medical Instrumentation.

National Academy of Medicine. 2018. Procuring digital interoperability in health care: A meeting of the Executive Leadership Network for a Continuously Learning Health

System, of the NAM Leadership Consortium for a Value & Science-Driven Health System. Available from: https://nam.edu/programs/value-science-driven-health-care/procuring-digital-interoperability-health-care-agenda-recordings/.

National Quality Forum. 2017. A measurement framework to assess nationwide progress related to interoperable health information exchange to support the National Quality Strategy. Available from: http://www.qualityforum.org/Publications/2017/09/Interoperability_2016-2017_Final_Report.aspx.

National Research Council. 2012. *Continuing innovation in information technology.* Washington, DC: The National Academies Press. Available from: https://doi.org/10.17226/13427.

National Research Council and Institute of Medicine. 2013. *US health in international perspective: Shorter lives, poorer health.* Washington, DC: The National Academies Press.

Oemig, F., and R. Snelick. 2016. *Healthcare interoperability standards compliance handbook.* Springer.

Office of the National Coordinator for Health Information Technology. Certified Health IT Product List. Available from: https://chpl.healthit.gov/, accessed June 4, 2018.

Office of the National Coordinator for Health Information Technology. 2014. Transitions of care (TOC) measures in the stage 2 Summary of Care Objective. Available from: https://www.healthit.gov/sites/default/files/transitions_of_care_toc.pdf.

Office of the National Coordinator for Health Information Technology. Health IT Playbook. Available from: https://www.healthit.gov/playbook/

Office of the National Coordinator for Health Information Technology. 2016. EHR contracts untangled: Selecting wisely, negotiating terms, and understanding the fine print.

President's Council of Advisors on Science and Technology. 2010. Realizing the full potential of health information technology to improve healthcare for Americans: The path forward. https://obamawhitehouse.archives.gov/sites/default/files/microsites/ostp/pcast-health-it-report.pdf.

Raghupathi, W., and V. Raghupathi. 2014. Big data analytics in healthcare: Promise and potential. *Health Information Science and Systems* 2:3.

Rahurkar, S., J. R. Vest, and N. Menachemi. 2015. Despite the spread of health information exchange, there is little evidence of its impact on cost, use, and quality of care. *Health Affairs* 34(3):477–483.

Rhoads, J. G., T. Cooper, K. Fuchs, P. Schluter, and R. P. Zambuto. 2009. Medical device interoperability and the Integrating the Healthcare Enterprise (IHE) initiative. *Biomedical Instrumentation & Technology* 21.

Romig, M., S. P. Tropello, C. Dwyer, R. M. Wyskiel, A. Ravitz, J. Benson, M. A. Gropper, P. J. Pronovost, and A. Sapirstein. 2015. Developing a comprehensive model of intensive care unit processes: Concept of operations. *Journal of Patient Safety*.

Strongwater, S., and T. H. Lee. 2016. Are EMRs to blame for physician burnout? *NEJM Catalyst*. Available from: https://catalyst.nejm.org/electronic-medical-records-blame-physician-burnout/.

Tuckson, R. V., M. Edmunds, and M. L. Hodgkins. 2017. "Telehealth." *New England Journal of Medicine* 377(16):1585–1592.

United States Government Accountability Office. 2010. Group purchasing organizations: services provided to customers and initiatives regarding their business practices. Available from: https://www.gao.gov/new.items/d10738.pdf.

Weininger, S., M. B. Jaffe, M. Robkin, T. Rausch, D. Arney, and J. M. Goldman. 2016. The importance of state and context in safe interoperable medical systems. *IEEE Journal of Translational Engineering in Health and Medicine* 4:2800110.

West Health Institute. 2013. The value of medical device interoperability: Improving patient care with more than $30 billion in annual health care savings. Available from: http://patientsafetymovement.org/wp-content/uploads/2016/02/Resources_Reports_Value_of_Medical_Device_Interoperability.pdf.

Appendix A

PROCURING INTEROPERABILITY TECHNICAL SUPPLEMENT

CONTRIBUTIONS AND ACKNOWLEDGMENTS

The development of the Technical Supplement is led by the Johns Hopkins University Applied Physics Laboratory, Alan D. Ravitz, Scott A. Gearhart, Kara L. Touhey, Robert A. Stoll, John F. Barnes, Thomas A. Longstaff, Conrad J. Grant, Ian M. Courtney, Candace D. Selig, Dan M. Portwood, and Tammy L. Tober.

Guidance and insights were provided by the following:

- Ed Cantwell, Center for Medical Interoperability
- Saad Chaudry, Johns Hopkins Medicine (former)
- Stan Huff, Intermountain Healthcare
- Jeff Rinda, Hospira
- Kate Lighty, Johns Hopkins Medicine
- Simon Mathews, Johns Hopkins Medicine
- John Pirolo, Ascension
- Larry Rammuno, Sibley Memorial
- Manish Shah, Community Health Systems
- Robert Snelick, National Institute of Standards and Technology (NIST)

TABLE OF CONTENTS

LIST OF ILLUSTRATIONS

SUMMARY OF THE TECHNICAL SUPPLEMENT

The five priorities for action described in the main text of the NAM special publication outline key steps organizations can take to advance the adoption of interoperability within the health care industry. This Technical Supplement complements the main text by describing a tangible approach by which health care organizations can define requirements and align their purchasing strategies to achieve system-wide interoperability.

The Technical Supplement is divided into four sections. Section 1 describes an overarching framework and implementation strategy for purchasing interoperable systems. It provides a step-by-step procurement specification process for organizations to follow when purchasing interoperable technology and then establishes guidance for making procurement decisions at each interoperability tier.

Each of the succeeding sections builds on the concepts in Section 1 by providing additional detail, examples, or case studies. Section 2 describes an example approach commonly used in systems engineering to identify priority interoperability requirements through the use of an N-squared diagram, a tool for cataloguing and prioritizing complex interactions of software, hardware, and people. Section 3 takes the procurement specification process one step further by providing examples of interoperability specification language, and finally, Section 4 describes two relevant case studies from nonhealth care industries that have tackled similar interoperability challenges.

Adopting a systematic and aligned approach to procurement across the industry enables the purchasing power of participating institutions to align, resulting in a market transformation—one where interoperability becomes inherent within health care technology. Health care organizations must embrace and reward those suppliers who are willing to demonstrate the principles of interoperability and openness. This Technical Supplement provides tools and terminology intended to assist facilities with that goal.

Technical Supplement—Section 1

IMPLEMENTATION STRATEGY FOR PURCHASING INTEROPERABLE SYSTEMS

Procuring interoperable solutions requires a common understanding of the terms *interoperability* and *openness*. In the context of health information technology, the 21st Century Cures Act defines "interoperable" information technology as that which "(A) enables the secure exchange of electronic health information with, and use of electronic health information from, other health information technology without special effort on the part of the user; (B) allows for complete access, exchange, and use of all electronically accessible health information for authorized use under applicable State or Federal law; and (C) does not constitute information blocking" (21st Century Cures Act, H.R. 34, 114th Congress, 2016). This definition highlights the benefit of shared information, implying that the automated exchange of data reduces human workload and the potential for errors associated with manual data transactions. Achieving an effective interoperability implementation is a complex process dependent on not only data quality, usability, security, and privacy but also culture, governance, and infrastructure. Effective interoperability enables organizations to achieve meaningful goals that include improved outcomes, fewer patient harms, and overall improved value.

System interoperability can imply a desire for system "openness." In an open design—often referred to as open architecture (OA)—one subsystem can be replaced with minimal effect on other subsystems as long as the replacement meets the open architecture specifications. For example, a hospital can replace or upgrade its laboratory information system (a subsystem) to a different vendor without affecting other subsystems such as the pharmacy, billing, or EHR. In the most successful open architecture applications, exchanging one subsystem for another has no effect on system integration. A full or partial open architecture implementation has the potential to ease integration workload and costs associated with replacing or upgrading a system or subsystem. Consequently, individual subsystems can be upgraded on a more frequent basis, enabling managed obsolescence and new capability insertion (DoD Open Systems Architecture Data Rights Team, 2013).

One means by which to increase system openness is adherence of connected subsystems to an interface standard and a well-defined open architecture setting the foundation for an open business model where organizations compete in the procurement process based largely on the performance and cost of their individual products (or subsystems) rather than on how information is exchanged between subsystems. (Section D describes how the US Navy transformed its procurement approaches for submarines and robotics, respectively, into open business models.) Most efforts at improving openness in health care systems to date have focused on adoption of standard health data and information interfaces, and there have been efforts to provide guidance for interoperability-related contract language (MD FIRE, 2017; SMART on FHIR, 2017; Office of the National Coordinator for Health IT, 2016; Office of the National Coordinator for Health IT, 2012) but more progress is needed.

The modular open system architecture (MOSA) approach realizes the full potential of OA. In MOSA, standardization goes beyond subsystem interfaces. A MOSA specification represents a system as a framework of interconnected modules where each module's interfaces, essential functions, and performance characteristics are clearly specified. A personal computer is an example of a MOSA implementation where the mouse, display, and keyboard are modules that must comply with certain essential requirements to achieve plug-and-play capability. Vendors competing to supply a particular module can offer unique features and cost savings to differentiate their product from competitors, but their product must comply with MOSA specifications.

Note that two subsystems can be interoperable (i.e., they can exchange information and use that information) and not be "open" as defined above. For example, a single subsystem supplier may use a nonstandard proprietary interface to connect with another subsystem. In this case, the two subsystems may be interoperable; however, if one subsystem is replaced with a subsystem from an alternate vendor, the legacy system must be modified to accommodate the different interface of the replacement. Consequently, replacing one subsystem might necessitate significant and costly modifications of the other. Herein, the use of the term *interoperability* also assumes the desire for openness.

INTEROPERABLE HEALTH CARE TECHNOLOGY PROCUREMENT FRAMEWORK

Using procurement to drive advances in interoperability across the industry requires synergy of health care organizations on a common procurement framework. Across many diverse, geographically dispersed, independently owned, and commercially developed health care systems and devices there is no single overarching authority or government entity that coordinates, controls, and funds the comprehensive changes required to achieve interoperability across the entire health care system. The government plays an important role in portions of the landscape, establishing guidance, policy, regulations, and funding development of interoperability enablers such as health data exchange standards. Even so, the hard work and resources needed for success falls to enlightened hospital executives and staff, forward-thinking health care system and device suppliers, and many others as part of a coalition of the willing.

There are no effortless solutions to achieving interoperability. Long-term vision, leadership commitment, a technical knowledgebase, and, perhaps most of all, persistence will be required for a health care organization to make progress. At the same time, numerous organizations have made great strides in the field of interoperability, which can be used to both make the individual hospital's task easier and move the industry forward. *Figure A1-1* shows the common foundation from which each hospital can build their procurement strategy. That foundation comprises work done by organizations such as the Office of the National Coordinator for Health IT (ONC), the National Institute of Standards and Technology (NIST), Integrating the Healthcare Enterprise (IHE), Health Level Seven International (HL7), Institute of Electrical and Electronics Engineers (IEEE), the Center for Medical Interoperability (CMI), and others.

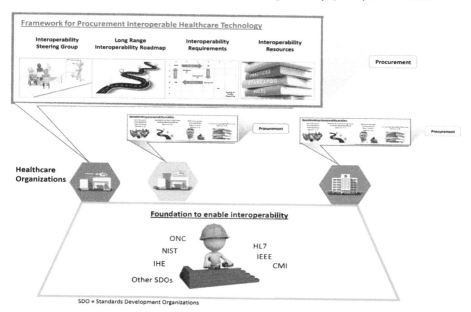

FIGURE A1-1 Framework for Procuring Interoperable Health Care Technology
SOURCE: Johns Hopkins University Applied Physics Lab, 2018

Although this foundation is available, health care organizations may not consistently specify their approach and RFP language clearly to realize the benefits of interoperable and open systems. To drive the industry toward interoperability, each health care organization (represented by the colored hexagons in *Figure A1-1*) must align four primary elements of a procurement framework. These elements, illustrated in *Figure A1-1* are as follows:

- An interoperability steering group: A group within each health care organization that develops strategic guidance on interoperability through setting priorities, coordinating, and overseeing IT acquisition activities across the organization. This steering group could be established anew or be formed within an existing steering committee overseeing the IT infrastructure and/or procurement. In addition to leading interoperability transformation within the organization, the group represents the organization in collaborating with other organizations throughout health care on resource sharing and collective learning.
- Long-range interoperability road map: A multiyear procurement plan that describes incremental objectives for improving interoperability and system openness.
- Interoperability needs identification process: The documentation and visualization of the complex information and workflow interactions in a health care setting, and the translation of these to interoperability needs for new or upgraded health care systems.
- Interoperability procurement specification process: The translation of interoperability needs to procurement specifications in RFPs leveraging various health system data exchange standards and supporting resources.

The resources produced through multiorganizational collaborations should be a shared resource across the field. In many cases, however, local tailoring of these resources will likely be required, since not all organizations or facilities are identical in terms of their care for patients, policies, procedures, and procurement priorities. Also described in *Figure A1-1* is the role of the industry. Health care organizations and facilities will use the public domain resources produced by the interoperability steering group to procure interoperable solutions from industry. Accordingly, the industry must conform to the policy, standards, and profiles that form the foundation for interoperability.

INTEROPERABILITY STEERING GROUP

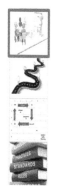

A senior level, CEO-mandated interoperability steering group is central to the organization's governance infrastructure to enhance interoperability and optimize the organization's investment in health IT acquisition (Selva and Katz, 2017). The interoperability steering group will ideally be a standing organizational committee supported by and accountable to the health care organization's top leadership. While some organizations may form a new standalone steering group, others may appoint a team of related capacity within their existing purchasing steering committee structure. Nevertheless, this senior-level committee serves as the "organizational champion" that motivates, oversees, coordinates, and periodically evaluates the procurement framework. This group should work with diverse stakeholders across the organization—including clinical departments (e.g., cardiology, emergency department, pathology, and so on), clinical/biomedical engineering, hospital administration, billing and revenue operations, and IT—to provide coordination and reduce fragmentation and silos. For example, this group can curate common interoperability specification languages that are consistent with the organization's visions, missions, and target outcomes. This group also serves as a liaison in participating in external consortium efforts to drive industry-wide interoperability.

The responsibilities of the interoperability steering group may vary by organization but should include the following:

- Work with stakeholders across the organization to identify common needs and workflow challenges, as well as unique service-specific circumstances related to data exchange requirements for care delivery;
- Develop concrete objectives and top priority clinical use cases regarding interoperability in the organization's procurement processes, including the development of a long-range interoperability road map;
- Identify interoperability priorities and form implementation plans across the organization's various procurement activities;
- Develop or curate common interoperability requirement language that may be used by multiple services and technology types, and oversee the adoption of best practices in procurement processes across the organization;
- Stay abreast of the latest advances in interoperability, data exchange standards, and industry-wide best practices across the macro-, meso-, and micro-tiers;

- Oversee the translation and customization of shared or open-source platforms or interoperability profiles to unique local contexts;
- Set performance metrics on progress over time and consistently measure them; and
- Represent the organization in external consortium efforts to promote information sharing, consensus building, and the establishment of common resources.

LONG-RANGE INTEROPERABILITY ROAD MAP

As described in earlier sections of this publication, health care organizations should have a multiyear procurement strategy, and this plan should include a road map that sets the vision for improving interoperability and system openness within the organization. The long-range interoperability road map provides guideposts for planned adjustment and/or transformation in the procurement practice that, over time, aims to move the organization closer to the vision.

This road map should be a living document based upon the best available information, adapting to both internal and external changes that influence procurement priorities of the organization. The interoperability steering group will develop the road map through engagements with stakeholders to understand their interoperability needs and identify opportunities to improve workflow and outcomes. To maintain visibility, focus, and relevance, the interoperability steering group should communicate the road map within the health care organization and continuously seeking feedback toward procuring interoperable solutions. Along with the organization's multiyear procurement plan, the road map should be updated at least annually to keep pace with technological developments in the field as well as evolving organizational needs.

INTEROPERABILITY NEEDS IDENTIFICATION PROCESS

The interoperability steering group should engage their organization's health care system stakeholders at least annually to identify needs and opportunities for making systems more interoperable and open, and subsequently to reflect them in updates of the interoperability road map. Note that this is more than a simple polling process. A single hospital unit includes many interactions between technology and staff; an entire hospital multiplies the number of interactions enormously. Comprehending and tracking all these interwoven and interdependent interactions can be daunting, yet understanding these relationships is essential to identifying interoperability needs and opportunities that drive a procurement strategy. Because of this complexity, it is not likely that stakeholders will simply submit their respective lists of interoperability requirements; rather, the interoperability steering group must lead the stakeholders through a series of methodical design development exercises from which these needs can be distilled.

The field of engineering offers many diagramming tools that may help organizations grapple with their respective interoperability challenges. These tools include diagrams such as flowcharts, block diagrams, and technical illustrations such as the family of diagrams defined by Unified Modeling Language (Object Management Group Unified Modeling Language, 2017) or SysML (Object Management Group Systems Modeling Language, 2017). One of the tools routinely used by systems engineers in industries such as space and military system development is the N-squared diagram (*Figure A1-2*, and Technical Appendix Section B). It is a technique used to document complex interactions among hardware or software systems (NASA, 2007), and it can afford health care the same benefits.

For example, the interoperability steering group can work with relevant stakeholders within the organization to develop an N-squared diagram of a care unit such as an intensive care unit (ICU).

At the start, the table shown in *Figure A1-2* would have all blank fields. The first step is entering the diagonal elements. These represent the entities (technologies, equipment, and people) that currently interact in the unit. The nondiagonal elements represent the interactions (including data exchange) between the various diagonal elements. By convention, any *output* of a diagonal element is identified in the *row* containing that element (shown by the green arrow). Any *input* of a diagonal element is represented in the *column* containing that element (shown by the blue arrow). Although there is no constraint on the type of interactions captured, a typical first step is to capture all manual (verbal and written) and electronic data transactions.

The process of developing the diagram motivates important discussions with stakeholders, including the following:

- Which processes currently rely most heavily on manual entry by staff, especially physicians and nurses?
- Which manually entered data fields have the greatest influence on care decisions and patient outcomes?
- Can any recurring data field (e.g., body weight, blood pressure, known allergies) be automated, thus minimizing manual entry or copying/pasting?
- Based on the nature of the data field, what is the level of data security and privacy protection needed?
- What are clinicians' needs for data accessibility, timeliness, and refresh rates?

- Do the data fields need to be shared with other clinical or administrative departments and/or external entities?
- What is the estimated staff time and resource cost of manual data exchange?

Once the diagram is populated, the layout of the information can reveal interoperability needs and opportunities that were not previously obvious. Lining up interoperability needs highlighted in the diagram with the organization's priorities informs the development of the Interoperability Road Map included in the organization's multiyear procurement plan (Section 1). Technical Supplement Section 2 demonstrates the development of an N-squared diagram for an endoscopy suite as a representative example of how to use this tool.

	A	B	C	D	E	F
1	EHR	Outputs →		D1		
2	↑ Inputs	Software #1		↓ Inputs		
3			Equipment #1			
4	A4	← Outputs		Device #1		
5						etc...
6						Quality & Safety Reporting

An Example N-Squared Diagram

SOURCE: Johns Hopkins University Applied Physics Lab, 2018

INTEROPERABILITY PROCUREMENT SPECIFICATION PROCESS

As described earlier, a particular need for interoperability involves the exchange of digital information among health care technologies. To acquire open system solutions, the health care organization must require the supplier to implement the interface between the technologies according to industry-accepted health data exchange standards. As of 2017, commonly used standards include the HL7 standards for exchange between health information systems, the IEEE 11073 standards for patient care devices, the SNOMED-CT medical diagnosis codes, the RxNORM medication codes, LOINC for laboratory and other observation identifiers, and a host of other notable health care-related standards.

BOX A1-1
Integration Profiles and Implementation Guides

A number of organizations have created *integration profiles* and *implementation guides* to promote adoption of health data standards while providing implementation instructions that reduce variability in applying the standards. The integration profiles and implementation guides developed by the IHE and HL7 International are perhaps the best known and widely accepted (Integrating the Healthcare Enterprise, 2016; HL7 International, 2017).

IHE has developed technical frameworks in 14 clinical domains such as anatomic pathology, cardiology, dental, endoscopy, and patient care devices (PCD). Each technical framework includes multiple *integration profiles*, each targeting particular interoperability needs. For example, the PCD Technical Framework includes the following:

- Device Enterprise Communications (DEC) profile—Integration of patient care devices to hospital information systems;
- Point-of-Care Infusion Verification (PIV) profile—Transfer of drug infusion parameters from a bedside computer-assisted medication administration (BCMA) system to an infusion pump;
- Alert Communications Management (ACM) profile—Communication of alerts to an alert-management system that communicates notifications via additional means to caregivers.

An IHE technical framework typically includes three documents ("volumes"): for each *integration profile*, Volume 1 describes the interoperability use cases addressed, the actors involved, and the required transactions between these actors (actors can be people such as nurses or technologies such as pulse oximetry); Volume 2 specifies the information exchanged between the actors and maps these to messages of the data exchange standard used; and Volume 3 describes how information exchanged will be consistently interpreted by all the actors (i.e., semantics mapping). Volume 1, which is less technical than Volumes 2 and 3, is of the most practical interest to a health care organization's interoperability steering group.

The IHE.net website lists resources and tools for vendors and users of health care information systems to help them integrate systems and share information more effectively. These free resources include user handbooks, case studies, technical frameworks, integration profiles, public comments, and educational webinars.

HL7 Implementation Guides are generally more focused and detailed, providing guidance for applying the HL7 family of standards to specific types of data exchanges with emphasis on transactions involving the EHR system. HL7.com lists well over 200 implementation guides spanning various HL7 versions. The website includes a search feature that helps users select the guides most relevant to a particular need.

SOURCE: Johns Hopkins University Applied Physics Lab, 2018

A data exchange standard specification can include multiple volumes of documentation, each having hundreds of pages of detailed technical information. Despite the term *standard*, it is often possible to apply or use a standard in a variety of different ways. Each vendor can interpret and develop a unique implementation of the standard to satisfy a similar purpose. Therefore, independent implementations of an interface that achieves the same purpose could be significantly different even while each complies with the same standard. Since open system solutions require identical or at least similar implementations, giving vendors latitude to use the standards as they choose leads to nonopen solutions industry-wide.

As a consequence, a health care organization must not only require candidate vendors to use particular data exchange standards for satisfying an interoperability need, but must also specify constraints on how the vendor is to implement these standards. Fortunately, organizations such as HL7 International, Integrating the Healthcare Enterprise (IHE), and Personal Connected Health Alliance (Personal Connected Health Alliance, 2017) have developed "guides" or "profiles" that provide instructions on how to implement various data exchange standards to satisfy different interoperability needs. *Box A1-1* describes these integration profiles and implementation guides in more detail. In addition, the Office of the National Coordinator for Health Information Technology's (ONC) Interoperability Standards Advisory (ISA) provides best-practice guidance on which data exchange standards, implementation guides, and integration profiles should be used (see description in *Box A1-2*).

BOX A1-2
ONC's Interoperability Standards Advisory

The ONC's Interoperability Standards Advisory (ISA) assists in the selection of standards, *integration profiles*, and *implementation guides* that best apply for specific data exchanges (i.e., technology X needs a specific data item from technology Y). The ONC ISA recommendations are based on the maturity of the standards process, the maturity on implementation, levels of adoption (including whether a standard or an *implementation guide* is federally required), associated costs, and the availability of testing tools (Office of the National Coordinator for Health IT, 2017a). The recommendations are grouped by "interoperability need"—a phrase that describes which data is involved in a transaction between senders and receivers. In practice, an early step for an interoperability steering group may include matching stakeholder needs with corresponding standards, *integration profiles*, and *implementation guides* in the ISA.

SOURCE: Johns Hopkins University Applied Physics Lab, 2018

Health care organizations of any size can leverage these resources in an organized fashion to translate their interoperability needs into procurement specification language. Consider the case in which a hospital requires a medical device to interface with the EHR system through a local network, thereby bypassing the need for manual data entry. The hospital's Interoperability Steering Group determines that upgrades of the EHR system are needed to accomplish this. The Request for Proposal (RFP) to the EHR vendor would include this statement:

> *The EHR system shall be upgraded to be compliant to the IHE Patient Care Device (PCD) Technical Framework, specifically to the Device Enterprise Communications (DEC) Integration Profile. Within the DEC profile, the EHR system shall have the role of the Device Observation Consumer.*

The language in this brief specification statement defines the interoperability need of the system, the data exchange standards to be used, and the constraints on how the standard should be implemented. Simple statements such as this can improve an organization's ability to stipulate interoperability in their procurement specifications. In addition to specifying interoperability and openness as an overarching goal, a health care organization would typically also prescribe functional requirements for the technology they are purchasing.

The interoperability steering group would work with the appropriate internal stakeholders to identify the information exchange needs. They can then provide guidance on the process of selecting data exchange standards, *implementation guides*, and *integration profiles*, and oversee the development of procurement specifications for new or updated systems or subsystems that must be interoperable with one or more other systems. *Figure A1-3* shows the key specification development steps leading to interoperability content for an RFP described as follows:

Step 1. Match interoperability need to interoperability resources. To execute this step, the interoperability steering group would seek recommendations from the ONC ISA and would research available integration profiles and implementation guides.

If an integration profile and/or implementation guide that align with a specific interoperability need *is* identified, then:

Step 2. Prescribe the integration profile(s) and implementation guide(s) vendors must use. The result is a statement included in the RFP. Refer to Technical Supplement Section 3.

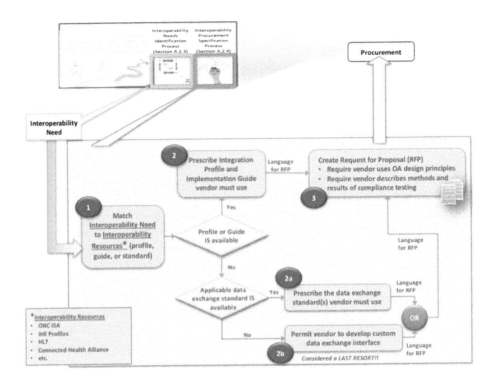

Interoperability Procurement Specification Process

SOURCE: Johns Hopkins University Applied Physics Lab, 2018

On the other hand, if there is *no* alignment between an interoperability need and a profile or implementation guide:

Step 2a. Prescribe the data exchange standard(s) vendors must use. Provide clarity of constraints of an *integration profile* or *implementation guide* for the vendor to implement the interfaces needed. Full disclosure of value sets, coconstraints, and other interface attributes is required.

Otherwise, in the case where no standard exists:

Step 2b. Permit vendor to develop custom interface. This may be necessary to meet a unique interoperability need, but all other options considered, it should be the choice of last resort.

Step 3. Create request for proposal—incorporate languages from Steps 2, 2a, and 2b, and:

- **Require vendor to use open architecture design principles.** See sample language in Technical Supplement Section C. Even in the case where a supplier must develop a custom interface, one that is consistent with a modular open system architecture is more likely to provide the basis for modular upgrades or new *integration profiles*.

- **Require vendor to describe methods and results of compliance testing.** The health care organization's proposal evaluation criteria should reward vendors who will perform best-practice standards and profile compliance testing.

Technical Supplement Section 3 describes examples of interoperability procurement language for several cases—(1) upgrade of a laboratory information system, (2) use-case-driven integration scenario in obstetrics, (3) integration of patient care devices with the EHR system, (4) request for specific functionality and interoperability capabilities or request for information, (5) modular open systems architecture language—that would result from following the process illustrated in *Figure A1-3*.

As a final note to this section, a health care organization's effective use of integration profiles and implementation guides in writing specifications is a discipline that can result in more open commercial products that reduce overall integration costs for new or upgraded capabilities. That said, some of these guiding resources may lack adequate specifics, forcing developers to make some design decisions. This leaves open the possibility of subtle variations in developer implementations that challenge achieving the ideal of plug-and-play system openness.

INTEROPERABILITY PROCUREMENT CONSIDERATIONS AND GUIDANCE

Taking into account the current state of the industry, this section will address general procurement guidance and considerations at each of the three interoperability tiers. No matter what type of system is being purchased, it can be useful to include a declaration statement at the start of the RFP to affirm the need for interoperability and security, as well as any unique missions and relevant clinical contexts worth noting.

RFP interoperability declaration statement

A health care organization should include in all RFPs for its technology acquisition a declaration statement that affirms the organization's commitment to seeking interoperable and open architecture solutions and favor vendors who offer those solutions. Even without further stipulation, the strength of many health care organizations making such statements may influence vendor business practices in a favorable direction. Such declarations also cultivate open-systems expectations and commitment within the organization. A sample declaration statement follows.

[Organization Name] is committed to promoting increased health system interoperability and openness, and, in our procurements, will favor vendors that support these objectives. Specifically, [Organization Name] will favor vendors who apply open architecture best practices:

- *Implement interfaces using best-practice data exchange standards, integration profiles, and implementation guides, and provide verification evidence of compliance of such;*
- *Provide full documentation disclosing interface design and functionality; and*
- *Provide full disclosure and breakdown of integration and test labor and costs.*

Health care organizations can refer to the *DoD Open Systems Architecture Contract Guidebook for Program Managers*, v1.1 (DoD Open Systems Architecture Data Rights Team, 2013) which provides open architecture best-practice language that can be directly quoted or paraphrased in the introductory sections of RFPs. Technical Supplement, Section 3 provides excerpts from the guidebook.

Here is another example source for introductory texts that may inform the health care organization's needs and motivations in procuring medical devices (MD FIRE Version 2.6, excerpt):

Objectives

We [Organization Name] intend to adopt and implement interoperability standards for medical device interconnectivity via our procurement actions. We also recognize that the necessary standards are not yet fully developed or widely implemented by medical equipment vendors. However, we believe that adoption of standards-compliant interoperable devices and associated systems (i) will enable the development of innovative approaches to improve patient safety, health care quality, and provider efficiency for patient care; (ii) will improve the quality of medical devices; (iii) will increase the rate of adoption of new clinical technology and corresponding improvements in patient care; (iv) will release health care delivery organization (HCDO) resources now used to maintain customized interfaces; and (v) will enable the acquisition and analysis of more complete and more accurate patient and device data, which will support individual and institutional goals for improved health care quality and outcomes.

Our goals are to (i) encourage the implementation of interoperability by compiling and presenting the evidence of present and projected clinical demand for the interoperability of medical devices; and (ii) encourage and facilitate the development and adoption of medical device interoperability standards and related technologies through HCDO procurement actions.

We are, therefore, including medical device interoperability as an essential element in our procurement process and in future vendor selection criteria.

CYBERSECURITY AND PRIVACY CONSIDERATIONS

Although interconnected systems afford great potential value, they can also lead to increased security-related risks if not properly mitigated (Palfrey et al. 2012). As in other industries, cybersecurity and privacy breaches can threaten trust and dampen willingness for data sharing. On the other hand, many legacy systems that operate in a silo have security vulnerabilities, and the system-of-systems environment may allow more shared resources devoted to assess risks and test mitigation and remediation strategies. In the context of the multitier model, it is vital to understand how interoperability may or may not affect the exposure, modification, and how these risks may be mitigated.

The NIST Cyber Security Framework (NIST, 2014) affords a tool leading to better understanding of the threat to interoperable health care systems, which tends to be secondary to other operational and functional requirements. To tackle security and privacy concerns, NIST's framework can provide a structure for defining functional and nonfunctional requirements for the acquisition of health care systems and components. The NIST cybersecurity framework provides a mechanism for health care organizations to:

- describe their current cybersecurity posture,
- describe their target state for cybersecurity,
- identify and prioritize opportunities for improvement within the context of a continuous and repeatable process,
- assess progress toward the target state, and
- communicate among internal and external stakeholders about cybersecurity risk.

NIST provides seven steps to establishing a cybersecurity program (NIST, 2014) and the notional information and decision flows of the framework can be applied at the macro-, meso-, and micro-tiers. More specific procurement considerations and guidance for each tier of interoperability follows. Each tier description will include brief security guidance.

MACRO-TIER CONSIDERATIONS AND GUIDANCE

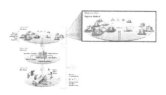

At the macro-tier level, the incentives offered over the past several years by the Affordable Care Act and Meaningful Use have resulted in Health Information Exchanges (HIEs) for information sharing across statewide health systems. Information at this level is shared mainly through the HL7 Clinical Document Architecture (CDA), a clinical document framework designed to be readable by both humans and computers (Oemig and Snelick, 2016). Given that connectivity exists and is spreading across the country, the discussion here focuses on reported challenges related to usability, quality, and security of the data exchanged.

Usability. One issue affecting usability of data exchanged at the macro-tier level is the sheer volume of information. For example, a very common type of document—a discharge summary—may be on the order of 50 pages. The number of documents, combined with the detail contained in each, can easily overwhelm a provider. Large volumes of data for each patient from each provider creates fragmented snapshots that are challenging for clinicians to absorb, potentially leading to misdiagnoses, unneeded testing, medical errors, and workload fatigue.

Next-generation HIEs may offer enhanced controls and capabilities that substantially reduce unnecessary data volume. Health care organizations should engage with regional and state HIE headquarters to understand requirements that may be levied on their individual systems to support these initiatives. Not all stakeholders require access to *all* of the patient's data. Stakeholders (clinicians, payers, researchers, and so on) should define default "views" specifying only the data they require—views that capture relevant data across all "fragments"—and assemble that data into a seamless view of the patient's record (i.e., a dashboard). The use of well-contrived views may reduce the amount of redundant information in the overall network. Research has been performed on methods for identifying, extracting, and aggregating unique content from multiple clinical documents on the same patient (Dixon et al. 2017). Individual hospitals should advocate further research in this area and monitor developments in commercially available predictive analytic algorithms and population health management tools.

Quality. Challenges with quality at the macro-tier include data accuracy, timeliness, and meaning (semantics). Data accuracy and completeness issues include wrong fields; incorrect use of terminology codes; missing data (empty fields); and invalid, unreadable, or inconsistent entries. The issues with data timeliness result in outdated, incorrect information. Variation in data semantics means different health information systems can use different dictionaries for various medical domains. Translation of services provided into documentation codes can vary among clinicians and among health care organizations.

Automated tools exist to validate the quality of CDA documents. ONC's C-CDA Scorecard, for example, provides implementers with industry best practice and usage. The Scorecard promotes best practices in C-CDA implementation by assessing key aspects of the structured data found in individual documents, as well as assessments on key areas for improvement. Health care organizations should push for the maturation and transitioning of these tools from today's stand-alone "test tools" into background real-time Continuity of Care Document (CCD)-quality check tools that can trigger alerts caused by data entry issues and can ensure that interoperability does not degrade system performance.

Finally, patient matching is a challenge that exists at all tiers and is especially important to quality at the macro-tier where records for a single individual may exist at multiple locations, provider organizations, and health systems that have yet to come together to form a comprehensive picture of a patient's care. Accurate patient-matching approaches is an active area of research, and given the importance of correct patient matching, health care organizations are encouraged to track developments in this area (e.g., the Sequoia Project, 2015; Office of the National Coordinator for Health IT, 2017a) and the subsequent effect on interoperability-related procurement language.

Cybersecurity and privacy. Security and privacy at the macro-tier starts with an identified threat model. In inter-facility information exchanges, there is a greater risk of data aggregation and exposure for a wide variety of nefarious purposes ranging from identity theft, fraud, and public exposure to deliberate life-critical modifications of data between facilities. Key mitigations at the macro-tier include common authentication/authorization between facilities, immutable logs to identify threat actors, and encrypted communications between facilities. Typically, these would be included in requirements for the use of information exchange gateways.

Envisioning the macro-tier of the future. The future of macro-tier interoperability can best be described by analogy: in the cellular communications industry today, regardless of whether one person uses Mobile Service Provider A and another uses Provider B, we expect to be able to communicate via voice and/or data (e.g., text message). In health care today, the situation is such that a hospital using Provider A can talk only to other Provider A hospitals. Organizations such as CommonWell Health Alliance (which is a trade association of health IT vendors that provides technical infrastructure to enhance patient matching, data query and retrieval, and person enrollment) are taking on the interoperability challenges at the macro-tier to support cross-vendor data exchange.

MESO-TIER CONSIDERATIONS AND GUIDANCE

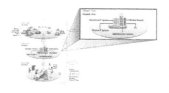

At the meso-tier, individual hospitals or clinics handle data and information associated with the EHR and other medical IT systems such as labs or pharmacies, and from operational and administrative IT systems such as food services or facilities, and admission/discharge/transfer (ADT). Data at this tier support the operation and administration of activities within the hospital, including clinical activities such as forming and maintaining a picture of the patient's care and condition over time; moving patients and supplies where they are needed; scheduling resources; and so on.

In the current state, hospitals tend to procure pharmacy, laboratory, and other health information technology (HIT) systems that integrate with their respective EHR. EHR vendors may include these HIT systems as part of their product line, which hospitals might opt to purchase as "bundled" services. Alternatively, hospitals might procure solutions for these HIT systems from other (i.e., non-EHR) vendors and pay additional costs for integrating these systems with the EHR. These custom integrations may involve vendor-to-vendor agreements that must be managed over the long term. Although interoperability between these systems can be achieved, neither of these approaches—bundled HIT or custom integrations—are open architecture solutions, and significant additional resource investments and maintenance will be required over the product's life cycle. These models of achieving meso-tier interoperability are typically not scalable and hence not sustainable as a long-term solution for the industry.

Requiring health IT vendors to use best-practice data exchange standards, integration profiles, and implementation guides for their products' interfaces is part of the strategy to achieving more open systems. A complicating factor at the meso-tier is that health IT systems are typically large-scale capital investments that health care organizations retain over many years. Given the lengthy life cycles for these systems and the disparity of types of systems, progress toward open systems must be incremental.

As an example, a hospital procures an upgrade to the laboratory information system (LIS) that includes the ONC Interoperability Standards Advisory (ISA)–recommended standard interface between the LIS and the EHR system. Suppose the hospital's EHR system is an older design that does not support the ONC Interoperability Standards Authority (ISA)-recommended LIS interface. The hospital could update the EHR system, but the current HIT budget might not support this. Another alternative is the use of an interoperability platform—(i.e., software and host computer systems that translate or transform a data interface from one form to another and facilitate the interconnection of different systems or subsystems). An **open architecture interoperability platform**, which is a data exchange framework composed of open and standard components and interfaces, is key to achieving the full benefit of interoperability and an open business model.

In this example, open architecture middleware serves as a bridge between the new LIS and legacy EHR, enabling retention of interoperability between the two.

At some point in the future when the EHR system is upgraded to the standard LIS-EHR interface, the open architecture middleware may be deemed unnecessary. Alternatively, the open architecture middleware might be retained to serve as the bridge interface to other systems having noncompatible interfaces within the same tier (e.g., meso-tier), but also across tiers (i.e., macro- or micro-tiers).

In addition to considering the potential benefits of open architecture middleware, health care organizations should monitor the progress of the new Fast Interoperability Healthcare Resources (FHIR) health data exchange standard. FHIR is the newest addition to the HL7 family of standards and includes many components of prior versions. The ONC has recognized the standard as being the "best available" one, and several major EHR system developers are incorporating early FHIR capabilities into their new systems.

FHIR bundles different types of health care information (e.g., administrative, clinical, financial, research, public health, and so on) into units called resources. HIT systems interconnect through a network and request and exchange resources with each other through a simple-to-use, web-based application programming interface (API). In this way, FHIR resources are available to all systems (though not always in real time), and a requesting system receives only the resources they request, making management of health-related data significantly easier and more reliable. Like other health data exchange standards, integration profiles and implementation guides are being developed for FHIR-based interfaces to satisfy various interoperability needs. FHIR development has largely focused on the macro- and meso- interoperability tiers, but use of FHIR at the micro-tier is also being considered (HL7 Wiki, 2017).

Cybersecurity and privacy. Within a facility, privacy is usually assured through physical access controls and traditional user authentication to critical systems. The automated information sharing between systems benefits from these factors. However, integration within a single vendor or between vendors may require a significant security infrastructure to ensure that all organizations sharing information use a common system authentication infrastructure to ensure that threats cannot gain access by disguising themselves as a legitimate organization for the purpose of violating privacy or modifying data within critical systems. Additionally, the increased use of wireless communications for meso-tier interoperability enables the connection of a threat that may be outside the security perimeter of the facility (e.g., in the parking lot). These facility authentication systems are historically difficult to configure and manage in a dynamic health care environment that includes automated department-to-department sharing, so it is important to address these growing complexities as increased meso-tier information sharing is established.

MICRO-TIER CONSIDERATIONS AND GUIDANCE

 The micro-tier represents the data exchanged at the point of care or from patients themselves through wearable devices or mobile health applications. These data may be disparate, ranging from verbal communications, medical record entries, device settings, images, and laboratory results to nontraditional data such as genomics information. Moreover, the data may or may not be generated and transmitted electronically. For example, some medical devices do not connect to any other systems, meaning a person must interpret the data from that device and manually enter it into other pertinent systems such as the EHR. The staff doing this interpretation and manual entry becomes a critical—though often inefficient—element in the information pipeline.

Having a clinician in the information pipeline is certainly essential, but in many cases, the individual is simply a conduit by which to transfer data or information. In such cases, reliance on manual transfer of information can undermine patient safety and caregiver productivity (American Hospital Association, 2018; Sinsky et al. 2016; Reves, 2003). Error in manually copied-and-pasted or entered data at the micro-tier is one of the root causes of data quality issues prevalent at the meso- and macro-interoperability tiers.

Therefore, a fundamental interoperability need at the micro-tier is the passing of data from medical devices into the enterprise information systems, thereby eliminating unnecessary manual data entry. The health care community has made some progress toward this end, but more progress is needed. *Figure A1-4* shows a number of point-of-care devices or device gateways (i.e., device hubs) sending data through a micro-tier interoperability platform that transforms the data into a standardized format for consumption by the EHR. Note that the configuration shown in *Figure A1-4* does not fully support an open business model. Ideally, a health care organization would desire the ability to replace or upgrade a particular device with another without affecting the rest of the system. With this ability to purchase in a modular fashion, they can potentially procure from a number of candidate vendors with products that allow plug-and-play. Because of the nonstandard interfaces depicted, which is common in the marketplace today, swapping out a technology with another that has a different interface would likely require major modifications to existing components or a new custom middleware platform. Interoperability platform products with ancillary data services are commercially available, but those relying solely on "middleware" products between proprietary interfaces can be extremely costly.

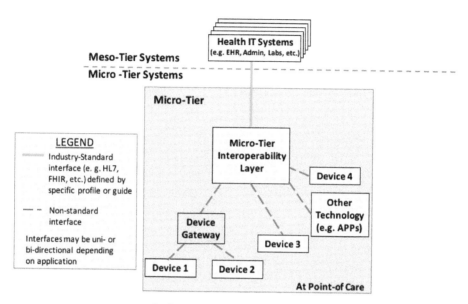

FIGURE A1-4 Electronic Data Transfer from Devices to the Health IT Systems That Does Not Support an Open Business Model

SOURCE: Johns Hopkins University Applied Physics Lab, 2018

Given the relatively frequent need to upgrade medical devices, it is perhaps at the micro- interoperability tier where health care organizations might benefit most from an open business model. *Figure A1-5* shows a fully open configuration where the interfaces between technologies are integrated through an open architecture interoperability platform using accepted standards. With this layer in place in this configuration, migrating any one of the components of the architecture to a new device or application can occur with lower development, integration, and testing expense, an ideal "plug-and-play" state.

As of 2017, the ONC recommends the IHE Device Enterprise Communications (DEC) integration profile for developing the gateway-to-EHR system interface. In procuring the micro-tier interoperability platform, a health care organization would require the vendor to be compliant with the IHE DEC profile. Additionally, the IEEE 11073 family of standards is the most mature work in standardized interfaces for certain classes of medical devices (IEEE Standards Association, 2017). Devices that IEEE 11073 currently addresses include:

- pulse oximeters,
- heart rate monitors,
- blood pressure monitors,
- thermometers,
- glucose meters,
- weight scales, and others.

Unfortunately, health care vendors of these types of devices have typically adopted only selected parts of IEEE 11073, notably the data dictionary (i.e., nomenclature). The parts of IEEE 11073 pertaining to communications transport, protocols, and message syntax, essential for standardizing device interfaces, have been largely unused. IEEE is working on augmenting the current IEEE 11073 family to include more flexible web-based communications methods. In recent years, the FHIR interface standard is being widely adopted for medical devices (HL7 Wiki, 2017).

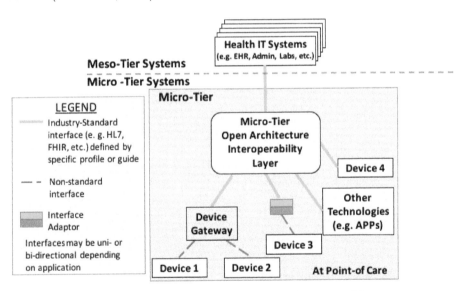

A Point-of-Care Device Configuration That Supports an Interim Open Business Model
SOURCE: Johns Hopkins University Applied Physics Lab, 2018

Health care organizations should favor device vendors who more fully comply with IEEE 11073 and other enhanced or new standards that follow. Given the relatively frequent need to upgrade medical devices, it is perhaps at the micro-tier interoperability where health care organizations might benefit most from an open business model. To realize this, device vendors need to support standard device interfaces.

Micro-tier interoperability increasingly includes health data that come from the patient portals, mobile health applications, and wearable personal care devices. The Personal Connected Health Alliance provides design guidance built upon the foundation of the IHE DEC integration profile and the IEEE 11073 family of medical device standards. The Personal Connected Health Alliance design guideline is an important resource that health care organizations can draw upon to aid in developing procurement specifications for open and interoperable systems. In addition, for portals, decision support, and other health IT (e.g., apps), the SMART on FHIR platform (*Box A1-3*) affords a means to capitalize on the growing adoption and maturity of the FHIR specification.

BOX A1-3
SMART on FHIR

For web-based technologies (e.g., other technologies noted in *Figure C-1*), the Substitutable Medical Apps, Reusable Technology (SMART) Platform project offers RFP language guidance to those health care organizations wishing to capitalize on the growing adoption and maturity of FHIR. The SMART Platform lays the foundation for flexible development and deployment of health information technology that can be integrated with existing health information technology such as electronic health records, portals, health information exchanges, and so on. The platform, an open, standards–based technology, led by Boston Children's Hospital and the Harvard Medical School, is built on four key components: FHIR, OAuth2, OpenID Connect, and HTML5 for structured data, scope and permissions, simple sign-in, and user-interface integration. In addition to these technology stack components, SMART on FHIR provides minimum RFP language needed to ensure existing health IT can support SMART on FHIR. This RFP language covers topics such as Data Access, Data Manipulation, Standards-based App Authorization, Identify Management, Workflow, and Intellectual Property. Notably, through a project called Argonaut, the five largest EHR vendors have joined forces with the SMART team and the HL7 organization to build SMART into the releases of their products, and to standardize the SMART API in HL7 specifications. In addition, there is a growing initiative called Devices on FHIR that aims to take a similar approach to ease the development and integration of devices into health IT systems.
SOURCE: Johns Hopkins University Applied Physics Lab, 2018

Section 3 of this Technical Supplement contains more details and resources on interface standards that can facilitate more specific procurement languages. In addition, entities such as the IHE, HL7, and the Medical Device Plug and Play (MD PnP) program (*Box A1-4*) also maintain resources related to integration profiles, sample languages, and clinical use cases for health care provider systems in navigating the marketplace through procurement specifications.

In the long run, however, the concept of a collaborative, open, API-based interoperability platform to allow the micro-tier to move toward a more vendor-neutral marketplace is embraced by many health care stakeholders. One

BOX A1-4

Medical Device "Plug-and-Play" (MD PnP) Interoperability Research Program

The Medical Device "Plug-and-Play" (MD PnP) Interoperability Research Program is based at the Massachusetts General Hospital (MGH) Department of Anesthesia, Critical Care, and Pain Medicine and Partners HealthCare System. Since its establishment in 2004, the program has focused on medical device interoperability as a foundation for patient safety, including the creation of complete and accurate EHRs and allowing third-party "app" development for clinical care and device management. The MD PnP program advocates for using high-priority clinical use cases to guide standards development and procurement of interoperable IT. Funding for the program largely came from research grants from the federal government (DoD, NSF, NIH, and DHS) and foundations.

Example research products from the program include the following:

1. OpenICE (Open-source Integrated Clinical Environment) is an initiative to create a community implementation of an Integrated Clinical Environment, connecting medical devices and clinical applications through both software/standards implementation and an architecture to enable new avenues of clinical research. OpenICE automates peer-to-peer node discovery, data publishing, and subscribing between nodes, as well as proprietary medical device protocol translation.

2. MD FIRE (Medical Device Free Interoperability Requirements for the Enterprise) comprises a white paper and sample RFP and contracting language developed by the MD PnP Program's Interoperability Contracting Requirements Working Group. MD FIRE RFP and contracting language is an open-source document and can be shared or reused under the Creative Commons Attribution–Share Alike license.

SOURCE: Johns Hopkins University Applied Physics Lab, 2018

BOX A1-5

Center for Medical Interoperability

Founded in 2013, the Center for Medical Interoperability (CMI) is a nonprofit organization whose board of directors is made up of leading health system CEOs with a common mission of simplifying and advancing data sharing among medical technologies and systems. Primarily focused on enhancing interoperability at points of care, it aims to serve as a centralized research and development lab to address technical challenges related to health care data security, connectivity, and interoperability. CMI membership is limited to health systems, individuals, and self-insured corporations but works with a variety of stakeholders, including medical device vendors, EHR vendors, standards development organizations, government/regulators, and other entities to advance the technical infrastructure required for data liquidity and interoperability.

Drawing on experience from other industries, such as banking/finance, cable, electrical power, and telecommunications, CMI is convening the purchasers of technology to agree upon a common architectural framework and corresponding technical interfaces for interoperability. As of 2018, there are three orchestrated technical campaigns: (1) Trusted Infrastructure and Medical Devices; (2) Connect Everything interoperability platform; and (3) a vendor-neutral, modular, and service-based Interoperability Platform Architecture. CMI aims to deliver these capabilities to the industry in the form of specifications, software reference implementations, and an interoperability testing and certification program.

SOURCE: Johns Hopkins University Applied Physics Lab, 2018

organization that operates in this space is the Center for Medical Interoperability (CMI, *Box A1-5*). The CMI's conceptual framework envisions a future of micro-tier health data exchange where an interoperability platform developed through collaborative research and development interfaces with devices as well as the application layer. If successful, such an API-based platform can enable more efficient procurement of plug-and-play technology, circumventing the frustration and cost challenges associated with closed middleware solutions that are prevalent today.

Interoperability is only a means to an end. Health care organizations should characterize the specific interoperability needs for these technologies, and demonstrate how enhanced connectivity improves patient care and workflow. Health care provider organizations can then leverage the processes outlined in this Technical Supplement to identify data exchange standards, best-practice integration profiles, and implementation guides that specifically target their interoperability needs for vendors to comply. As of now, some interoperability needs may require the vendor to build a custom interface as a last resort. In this case, the RFP should stipulate that the vendor demonstrate use of open architecture practices highlighted in Section 3 of this Technical Supplement, in particular full documentation and disclosure of the interface design.

Cybersecurity and privacy considerations. At the micro-tier, specific concerns take the form of secured and authenticated communications between individual devices. Within a single vendor, these security features may be enabled and be transparent to the use of the equipment, but when linking devices across vendors, there may be additional concerns that require more extensive configuration and maintenance. Open standards and security-enabled APIs will encourage security controls between devices, but the risk here is that the security controls may be disabled to facilitate rapid integration. Health care organizations are encouraged to review the imperatives, recommendations, and actions described by the Healthcare Industry Cybersecurity Task Force (PHE, 2017) related to medical devices and health IT systems. Some of the recommendations have long been implemented widely, such as requiring strong authentication and staff training on security and privacy protection. Other considerations may require additional governance and processes to secure legacy systems, improve transparency among developers and users, and employ strategic and architectural approaches to reduce physical breach or cyberattack of medical devices and health IT technologies. The Food and Drug Administration (FDA) also disseminates guidance on mitigating and managing cybersecurity threads and convenes experts on approaches to safeguarding medical devices and health IT systems.

CONCLUSION

Many health care organizations face constant challenges in adopting new capabilities and improving care when their devices and IT systems do not work together as an integrated system. Health care of tomorrow must develop an enterprise-wide architecture that enables system-wide interoperability to fuel a learning organization, as well as encouraging rapid development and adoption of technology innovations. In the interim, health care organizations must adopt a different approach in procuring technology that prioritizes interoperability with greater specificity. Health care organizations must commit to a requirements-driven approach for purchasing new technology that rewards interoperability, modularity, and openness. For many organizations, this means establishing a governance structure to coordinate and guide various internal efforts in leveraging existing implementation profiles and data standards in their procurement processes. Health care organizations must also work with standards development organizations, vendors, and other provider organizations to expand best practices and share resources. An industry-wide commitment toward this requirements-driven approach, driven by strategic partnerships among provider systems, patients, technology vendors, federal agencies, and other health IT societies, is the only viable path toward a safer, more efficient, and high-value health care enterprise.

Technical Supplement—Section 2

N-SQUARED DIAGRAM APPROACH TO IDENTIFYING INTEROPERABILITY REQUIREMENTS

The field of engineering offers many diagramming tools that may help organizations grapple with understanding their respective interoperability challenges. These tools include diagrams such as flowcharts, block diagrams, and technical illustrations such as the family of diagrams defined by Unified Modeling Language (Object Management Group Unified Modeling Language, 2017) or SysML (Object Management Group Systems Modeling Language, 2017). The N-squared diagram is a tool used in systems engineering to help organize interaction complexity. The tool is routinely used in industries such as space and military system development to identify interactions between hardware or software systems (NASA, 2007). At the most basic level, the N-squared diagram can be a convening tool that an organization's interoperability steering group uses to guide interoperability-focused conversations with clinical and operational stakeholders. Once the diagram is populated, the characteristic layout of the information can reveal interoperability needs and opportunities. The diagram is not only useful for understanding the organization's interoperability needs for procurement planning purposes, but can also be used more specifically to evaluate interoperability requirements for proposed new purchases. Model-based tools similar to NIST's prototype Architecture Development Facilitator (Fenves et al. 2007) can provide a framework for populating the N-squared diagram and visualizing the various interactions between the chosen set of components in the N-squared matrix. Further, several interaction and interoperability scenarios can be simulated using these model-based resources.

Figure A2-1 demonstrates the tabular layout of the N-squared diagram for a specific care unit (e.g., intensive care unit, or ICU). At the start, the table would have all blank fields. The first step is entering the diagonal elements as shown. These represent the entities (technologies, equipment, and people) that interact in the unit, presuming the initial focus is on characterizing the current state. The nondiagonal elements are then filled in, representing the interactions between the various diagonal elements. There is no restriction on the type of interactions to be captured, but a typical first step is to include all manual (verbal and written) and electronic data transactions when possible. Although the description here focuses on a hospital unit, the diagonal elements entered could relate to interactions at any of the interoperability tiers discussed previously (macro-, meso-, or micro-tier).

	A	B	C	D	E	F
1	EHR					
2		Software #1				
3			Equipment #1			
4				Device #1		
5					Staff Member #1	
6						etc.

N-Squared Diagram

SOURCE: Johns Hopkins University Applied Physics Lab, 2018

Figure A2-2 shows the convention for nondiagonal elements. An output of a diagonal element is marked across the corresponding row (shown by the green arrow), and an input of a diagonal element is marked across the corresponding column (shown by the blue arrow). Using the cell "D1" as an example, the content of this element would include any output data from the EHR that are input to Device 1 (such as patient height and weight data). Likewise, element "A4" shows output from Device 1 that becomes input to the EHR.

Once the diagram is filled, each intersecting point requires further details on how this document is exchanged and what the current interaction method is. Are clinical staff manually transferring the data, or is the process electronic/automated? Manual data interactions offer opportunities for improvement, but there may be several or even numerous incidences that are identified. The organization's interoperability steering group can provide high-level guidance on prioritization over the short run and the long run. Factors to consider for prioritization may include patient safety and quality concerns, burden on efficiency and workflow, and costs. How an organization's interoperability steering group

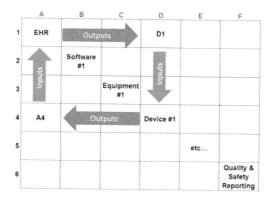

N-Squared Interactions
SOURCE: Johns Hopkins University Applied Physics Lab, 2018

weighs these prioritization factors will certainly be context specific. It is, therefore, important for the interoperability steering group to play a coordinating role, engaging relevant stakeholders to drive a collaborative outcome. At the organizational level, the interoperability steering group should establish a knowledge base and apply a coherent strategic direction on interoperability across various procurement activities.

The N-squared diagram may seem cumbersome, but most of the efforts are concentrated at the beginning. Once a baseline mapping of the current state of data exchanges is complete, future iterations are likely to require only incremental modifications.

N-SQUARED DIAGRAM APPLIED TO AN ENDOSCOPY SUITE

The following example applies the N-squared diagram to an endoscopy unit. The endoscopy suite, which provides diagnostic and therapeutic procedures like colonoscopy (both routine and emergency), is representative of the broader ambulatory procedure environment where numerous types of procedures and clinical scenarios take place. This example demonstrates the complex interactions among patients, technology, and staff and the need for tools to help understand and prioritize interoperability needs.

Building the framework

Step 1: Identify the entities that need to transfer information or data. These entities may include:

- IT systems (e.g., EHR, other clinical or administrative systems);
- equipment (e.g., radiology, anesthesiology, bedside monitoring);
- medical devices;
- people (e.g., patient, doctors, nurses, technicians); and
- reporting systems (e.g., quality or safety reporting, public health reporting).

Step 2: Place these systems along the diagonal of the table. *Figure A2-3* shows an example within a hypothetical endoscopy suite.

	A	B	C	D	E	F	G	H	I	J	K	L
1	Electronic Health Record (EHR)											
2		Endoscopy Report Software (ERS)										
3			Endoscope & Processor									
4				Displays / Monitors								
5					Image/Video Storage Computer							
6						Manual Endoscope Cleaning						
7							Disinfection Machine					
8								Nurse				
9									Doctor			
10										Technician		
11											Receptionist	
12												Quality/Safety Reporting

N-Squared Diagonal Entries

SOURCE: Johns Hopkins University Applied Physics Lab, 2018

Step 3: Start in the upper left-hand corner, above the diagonal line (cell B1). This cell represents one of two interactions between the EHR and the endoscopy report software (ERS) systems. In this cell, enter the information coming from the EHR (output) and entering the ERS (input). In this example, patient orders and appointment information come from the EHR and enter the ERS system. Continue to fill out the remainder of the cells above the diagonal in a similar manner.

Step 4: Return to the upper left-hand corner, but now focus below the diagonal line, and repeat the process described in Step 3. This time, cell A2 represents the information coming from the ERS (output) and entering the EHR (input). For example, the ERS system needs to send procedure reports and endoscopic images to the EHR. Continue to complete the boxes below the diagonal line.

IDENTIFY KEY RELATIONSHIPS AND OPPORTUNITIES FOR IMPROVEMENT

Step 5: Once the key data interactions are completed, each box or interaction should be marked as a manual or automatic interaction. In *Figure A2-4*, manual interactions are marked in red, and automatic or electronically driven interactions are marked in green.

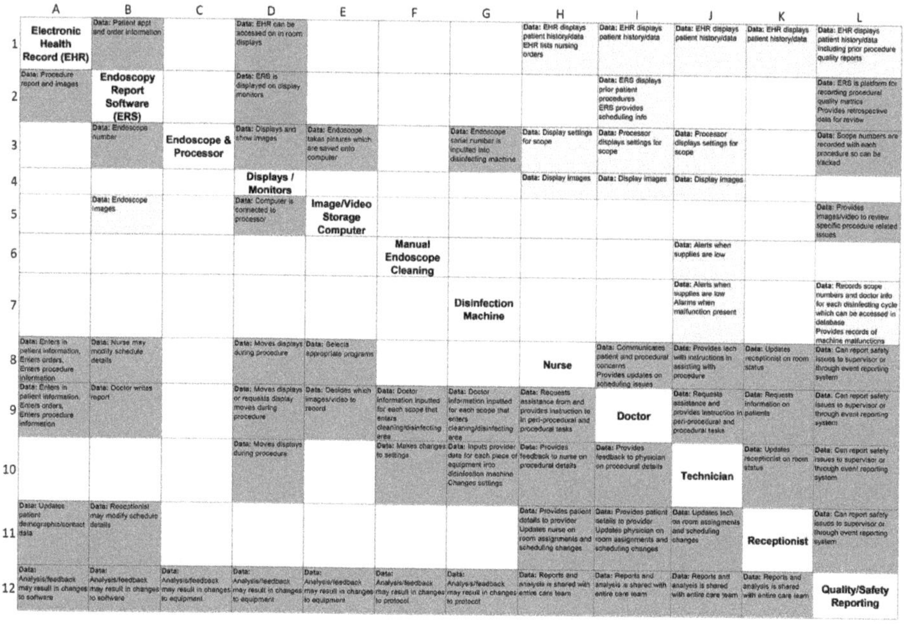

FIGURE A2-4 N-Squared Automatic Versus Manual Interactions
SOURCE: Johns Hopkins University Applied Physics Lab, 2018

Step 6: Identify manual interactions as possibilities for enhancing digital interoperability. With guidance from the interoperability steering group, prioritize among these interactions based on urgency or potential effects on safety, quality, or cost.

Step 7: *Figure A2-5* focuses on a subsection of the N-squared diagram (cells A1 to G7). Assume the prioritization process highlights two specific areas for improving interoperability (marked yellow and blue):

1. The yellow cells identify the need for the EHR to be more interoperable with the ERS system. After consulting with the interoperability steering group, the staff identifies this interaction as consistent with the IHE Endoscopy supplement, which are available for trial implementation.

2. The blue cells represent the need to link the endoscope number from the ERS to a specific patient and to the disinfection system. This is a matter of patient safety, not just workflow efficiency. Unfortunately, the staff cannot identify any existing integration profile or implementation guide.

	A	B	C	D	E	F	G
1	Electronic Health Record (EHR)	Data: Patient appt and order information Priority: Medium		Data: EHR can be accessed on in room displays Priority: Medium			
2	Data: Procedure report and images Priority: High	Endoscopy Report Software (ERS)		Data: ERS is displayed on display monitors Priority: Medium			
3		Data: Endoscope number Priority: Medium	Endoscope & Processor	Data: Displays and show images Priority: Medium	Data: Endoscope takes pictures which are saved onto computer Priority: Low		Data: Endoscope serial number is inputted into disinfecting machine Priority: Medium
4				Displays / Monitors			
5				Data: Computer is connected to processor Priority: Low	Image/Video Storage Computer		
6						Manual Endoscope Cleaning	
7							Disinfection Machine

N-Squared Prioritized Opportunities

SOURCE: Johns Hopkins University Applied Physics Lab, 2018

SUMMARY

The N-squared diagram serves as a tool for clinical and engineering teams to take inventory, in order to align their interoperability vision and requirements. Health care organizations may use tools such as this to establish a baseline for a particular service unit or a care path. Completing the initial draft of the N-squared diagram requires more work, but modifying the baseline and tracking updates over time should be less time intensive. This assessment process should be teamwork, including clinical and IT/engineering staff. The involvement and guidance from the interoperability steering group ensures that high-level vision and mission are instilled in the process. The goal of the N-squared exercise is to understand the full requirements of the end user and facilitate communication between information technology, clinical staff, and patients.

Technical Supplement—Section 3

EXAMPLES OF INTEROPERABILITY SPECIFICATION LANGUAGE

UPGRADE OF A LABORATORY INFORMATION SYSTEM (LIS)

This example addresses the need of a hospital to upgrade their laboratory information system (LIS). The specification language below pertains to required interoperability between the hospital's legacy EHR system and the new LIS. Note that the RFP would typically include other specification statements not considered here, such as addressing the features, capabilities, and cybersecurity provisions of the system.

Under the guidance of the interoperability steering group, the procurement team begins the specification development process by reviewing the existing IHE Technical Frameworks (IHE, 2016). They find that the Laboratory Testing Workflow (LTW) integration profile in the IHE Pathology and Laboratory Medicine Technical Framework addresses the interface between the LIS and the EHR system, where the former is termed the *order filler* and the latter the *order placer*. The LTW profile identifies three pertinent information "transactions": (1) lab orders from the EHR system to the LIS, (2) lab test results from the LIS to the EHR, and (3) order status from the LIS to the EHR system.

Next, the interoperability steering group facilitates the consultation of the ONC Interoperability Standards Advisory (ISA) to determine if the ISA addresses the information transactions above. The ISA recommends two HL7 2.5.1 Implementation Guides as best-of-breed for transactions (1) and (2). Confirming that the hospital EHR system is compliant with the guides, the LIS RFP references these implementation guides identified. Because the ONC ISA does not provide a recommendation for the interface for transaction 3 above, the interoperability steering group may advise referencing the IHE LTW profile directly in the RFP.

Sample RFP language follows.

Interoperability with the Legacy EHR:

The vendor's LIS shall receive laboratory orders from a legacy EHR system that is compliant with the HL7 Version 2.5.1 Implementation Guide: S&I Framework Laboratory Orders from EHR, Release 1 DSTU Release 2—US Realm.

The vendor's LIS shall transmit laboratory results to a legacy EHR system in accordance with the HL7 Version 2.5.1 Implementation Guide: S&I Framework Lab Results Interface, Release 1—US Realm.

The vendor's LIS shall transmit the status of laboratory orders to a legacy EHR in accordance with the IHE Pathology and Laboratory Medicine Technical Framework, Laboratory Testing Workflow Integration Profile, where the LIS has the role of the order filler. The vendor shall include implementation of the order filler actor option "Report Facsimile for Order Group."

In the proposal, the vendor shall provide a statement of compliance to the requirements above that includes the specific LIS model and software version being proposed, the deployment date, specifics on how compliance was verified, and the evidence that the vendor or an independent certification agent can provide to support their compliance statement.

If the vendor's LIS is not, or only partially, compliant, with the requirements above, the vendor shall specify which requirements their system can meet and the evidence the vendor can provide to support this. The vendor shall give specifics of future upgrades to their system that will increase compliance with the requirements above. The proposal evaluation criteria will give credit to proposals that have partial compliance and/or have definitive future plans for increased compliance.

Note that this example makes no mention of the EHR system being compliant with the IHE profile for receiving order status from the LIS. If the EHR system is not compliant, the hospital could contract the EHR vendor to update the EHR system to make it compliant, in conjunction with the new LIS procurement. In some cases, the hospital may also procure an open architecture interoperability layer (preferably not a middleware with proprietary interfaces) that connects the new LIS's IHE compliant interface into a data exchange format that the EHR system can receive.

USE-CASE-DRIVEN INTEGRATION SCENARIO IN OBSTETRICS

An important interoperability use case at both the macro- and meso-tiers involves the passing of appropriate clinical information associated with a series of related episodes of care from one specific care setting to another within the organization's enterprise health information systems (e.g., the EHR).

For example, obstetrical patients will typically see a clinician (physician, nurse, midwife) in an ambulatory/office setting, deliver in a hospital or freestanding birthing center, and return for postpartum care in the clinical office setting afterward. Depending on the organization, that may take place both within and external to the enterprise health IT. Additionally, obstetrical patients may encounter illnesses, injuries, or complications of pregnancy while traveling outside the area of their usual care.

After the obstetrical care-use case is identified as a priority, the interoperability steering group may be tasked with including interoperability specifications in procurement contexts such as these:

- Upgrading of legacy Labor and Delivery niche EHR system
- Ensuring full (bidirectional) data liquidity and connectivity between the Labor and Delivery EHR system(s) and the Enterprise EHR
- Ensuring full data liquidity and connectivity between Labor and Delivery EHR and the enterprise quality reporting systems and registries
- Ensuring full data liquidity and connectivity between Labor and Delivery EHR systems and the pediatrician office EHRs for beginning the newborn EHR

The interoperability steering group consults the Integrating the Healthcare Enterprise (IHE) Antepartum and Labor and Delivery Profiles found in the IHE Patient Care Coordination (PCC) Technical Framework for specifying and implementing the interfaces associated with an interoperability middleware layer and/or an enterprise IT system such as the EHR.

The IHE library contains the following types of resources:

- **Profiles**—Organized sets of IHE actors and transactions to address specific patient care needs. Multiple IHE profiles may be implemented together to achieve more complex clinical workflows.
- **Actors**—Information systems or applications that produce, manage, or act on information in the context of an IHE profile. Each actor supports a specific set of IHE transactions. A given information system may support one or more IHE actors.
- **Transactions**—Exchanges of information between actors using messages based on established standards. Each transaction is defined with reference to a specific standard and additional detailed information.

Examples of procurement language follow.

For EHR system vendors (niche Labor and Delivery EHR or enterprise EHR systems):

The EHR system shall be upgraded to be compliant with the IHE Patient Care Coordination (PCC) Technical Framework Integration Profile Antepartum Summary (APS), where the EHR system has the role of the Content Consumer (APS) actor. The EHR system shall also be compliant with the Content Bindings with XDS, XDM, or XDR Integration Profiles in the IHE IT Infrastructure (ITI) Technical Framework, upon which various PCC profiles depend, and the EHR system has the role of the Content Consumer actor. The EHR system shall receive data from the Content Creator actor (originating Obstetrical EHR system) conforming to the IHE PCC APS profile and related obstetrical profiles (e.g., Antepartum Education [APE], Antepartum History and Physical [APHP] records, Antepartum Laboratory [APL], and Immunization Content [IC]). The EHR system shall also be required to support actor and transaction requirements in profiles bound to the aforementioned PCC profiles (e.g., Document Source actor in XDS).

The EHR system shall also be upgraded to be compliant with the IHE Patient Care Coordination (PCC) Technical Framework Integration Profile Labor and Delivery History and Physical (LDHP), and Labor and Delivery Summary (LDS), where the EHR system has the role of the Content Creator actor. The EHR system shall also be compliant with Content Bindings with XDS, XDM, or XDR Integration Profiles in the IHE IT Infrastructure Technical Framework, upon which various PCC profiles depend, and the EHR system has the role of the Content Creator actor. The EHR system shall send data to the Content Consumer actor (receiving ambulatory OB EHR system) conforming to the IHE PCC LDHP profile and LDS profile, and other related obstetrical profiles. The EHR system shall also be required to support actors and transaction requirements in profiles bound to the aforementioned PCC profiles (e.g., Document Source actor in XDS).

NEWBORN DISCHARGE SUMMARY

The EHR system shall also be upgraded to be compliant with the IHE Patient Care Coordination (PCC) Technical Framework Integration Profile Newborn Discharge Summary (NDS), where the hospital EHR system has the role of the Content Creator actor. The EHR system shall also be compliant with Content Bindings with XDS, XDM, or XDR Integration Profiles in the IHE IT Infrastructure Technical Framework, upon which various PCC profiles depend. The EHR system shall send data to the Content Consumer actor (receiving ambulatory pediatric EHR system) conforming to the IHE PCC NDS profile and other related profiles. The EHR system shall also be required to support actors and transaction requirements in profiles bound to the aforementioned PCC profiles (e.g., Document Source actor in XDS).

POSTPARTUM VISIT SUMMARY

The EHR system shall also be upgraded to be compliant with the IHE Patient Care Coordination (PCC) Technical Framework Integration Profile Postpartum Visit Summary (PPVS), where the hospital EHR system has the role of the Content Creator actor. The EHR system shall also be compliant with Content Bindings with XDS, XDM, or XDR Integration Profiles in the IHE IT Infrastructure Technical Framework, upon which various PCC profiles depend. The hospital EHR system shall send data to the Content Consumer actor (receiving ambulatory OB EHR system) conforming to the IHE PCC PPVS profile and other related profiles. The EHR system shall also be required to support actors and transaction requirements in profiles bound to the aforementioned PCC profiles (e.g., Document Source actor in XDS).

INTEGRATION OF PATIENT CARE DEVICES WITH THE EHR SYSTEM

An important interoperability use case involves the passing of data from sensors and devices into the organization's enterprise EHR system. This is in contrast to the practice of a nurse recording the device outputs on paper and manually entering them into a computer terminal—a practice that is inefficient and error prone.

In this example, suppose an organization identifies the need for a particular set of devices to pass data directly to the EHR system as part of a modernization initiative. In an earlier section, *Figure A1-5* shows the configuration supportive of an open business model, where a number of devices connect to the EHR system through various adapters using industry-standard interfaces. The interoperability steering group oversees the modernization initiative through enhancing interoperability specifications in RFPs, which may include:

• upgrading the legacy EHR system,
• curating and implementing an open architecture interoperability platform layer, and
• purchasing new devices.

A number of different courses of action are possible to implement the open business model concept illustrated in *Figure A1-5*. A representative approach, one relying on open standards, draws on the ONC ISA, which recommends the Device Enterprise Communications (DEC) Integration Profile found in the IHE Patient Care Device (PCD) Technical Framework for implementing the interface between the Open Architecture Interoperability Layer and Health IT Systems depicted in *Figure A1-5*. In addition, the ONC ISA identifies the IEEE 11073 family of standards as the best-of-breed for "push communication of vital signs from medical devices." The interoperability steering group consults the ONC ISA, which recommends the Device Enterprise Communications (DEC) integration profile found in the IHE Patient Care Device (PCD) Technical Framework for implementing the interface between an open architecture platform and the EHR. The ONC ISA identifies the IEEE 11073 family of standards as best-of-breed for "push communication of vital signs from medical devices" (the Food and Drug Administration also endorsed IEEE 11073 standards).[1]

As a reminder, some related IHE terms are as follows:

- *Transaction*—a particular information exchange
- *Actors*—systems or components involved in an information exchange
- *Dependent profile*—Some IHE integration profiles (such as DEC) require support services described by another integration profile. For example, when specifying the DEC profile, one also needs to specify the Consistent Time (CT) profile.

In addition, the interoperability steering group consults online resources developed by the MD PnP program and develops the following example procurement language:

For the EHR system vendor:

> *The EHR system shall be upgraded to be compliant with the IHE Patient Care Device (PCD) Device Enterprise Communications (DEC) profile where the EHR system has the role of the Device Observation Consumer (DOC) actor. The*

---

1   The National Committee for Clinician Laboratory Systems (NCCLS) issued a "Point of Care Testing" standard (POCT1-x) in 2001 and revised it in 2006. The purpose of this standard is to "allow users to integrate data seamlessly between hospital information systems and POC devices such as handheld glucose meters" (*CAP Today*, 2011). Adoption of this standard, however, is reportedly limited (*CAP Today*, 2011). Accordingly, for the illustrated example described here, we focus on the ONC guidance related to the IHE PCD Technical Framework.

EHR system shall also implement the Time Client actor in the Consistent Time (CT) Integration Profile found in the IHE IT Infrastructure Technical Framework. The EHR system shall accept messages from an IHE PCD DEC compliant Open Architecture Interoperability Platform serving as the Device Observation Reporter (DOR) actor. The EHR system shall receive, via the Open Architecture Interoperability Platform, data from the device types specified in Table 1 (not shown in this example).

For the Open Architecture Interoperability Platform suppliers:

The vendor shall provide an Open Architecture Interoperability Platform that conditions medical device data for input into the EHR system. The Open Architecture Interoperability Platform shall be compliant with the IHE Patient Care Device (PCD) Technical Framework Integration Profile Device Enterprise Communications (DEC) where the Open Architecture Interoperability Layer has the role of the Device Observation Reporter (DOR). The Open Architecture Interoperability Platform will implement the Time Client actor in the Consistent Time (CT) Integration Profile in the IHE IT Infrastructure Technical Framework. The Open Architecture Interoperability Layer shall interface with an IHE PCD DEC compliant EHR system serving as the Device Observation Consumer (DOC) actor.

The Open Architecture Interoperability Platform shall receive data from the device types and manufacturers listed in the enclosed table (not shown in this example). Open Architecture Interoperability Platform products that provide the option of communicating with the highlighted device types in Table 2 in compliance with IEEE 11073–20601 Optimized Exchange Protocol will be ranked higher as described in the proposal evaluation criteria [would be included elsewhere in the RFP].

Device Suppliers:

The vendor shall describe device products they can provide within the classes of devices specified in the enclosed table. For the device types highlighted in the table, products that communicate with an IHE PCD compliant Open Architecture Interoperability Platform having the role of the Device Observation Report (DOR) actor using a full implementation of the IEEE 11073 standard will receive higher ranking during the source selection process.[2]

---

2   The IHE PCD DEC Device Observation Reporter (DOR) uses HL7 V2.6 messaging, IEEE 11073 nomenclature and elements of the IEEE 11073 Domain Information Model (DIM). A significant and growing number of devices directly implement IHE, PCD, DEC, and AMC capability inside the device (personal communication, 2017) signaling wider adoption of the IHE approach.

Full IEEE 11073 implementation is defined here as compliance with IEEE 11073–10101, IEEE 11073–20601, and the appropriate device-specific standards IEEE 11073-104XX, where XX is the number corresponding to the device type. Full IEEE 11073 implementation also includes use of the Personal Connected Health Alliance design and interface guides. Devices that use adapters to convert nonstandard interfaces to be IEEE 11073 compliant are acceptable.

If devices do not fully comply with IEEE 11073, the vendor should specify the parts of the standard that their device(s) complies with. The supplier will identify evidence they can provide that supports their IEEE 11073 compliance assertions. Upon delivery of devices the vendor shall provide complete engineering documentation of the interfaces.

It is important to note that device vendors may indicate that they are compliant with the IEEE 11073 standard but, in reality, be compliant only with the nomenclature part of the standard (which is widely adopted). Open system solutions require compliance with all parts of the standard.

REQUEST FOR SPECIFIC FUNCTIONALITY AND INTEROPERABILITY CAPABILITIES OR REQUEST FOR INFORMATION

After the interoperability steering group identifies a specific medical device that can benefit from enhanced interoperability, it identifies sections of example RFP languages from the MD FIRE program (*Box A1-4*). Working closely with specific clinical departments seeking to replace their existing devices, the interoperability steering group helps customizing the following example RFP texts to request a complete description of specific functionality and interoperability capabilities from vendors. As noted by MD FIRE (MD FIRE Version 2.6, 2017), the actual content should be selected by the health care delivery organization as appropriate for their clinical, business, or technical requirements.

RFP Text Example 1: Request for specific functionality and interoperability capabilities

This text, excerpted from MD FIRE Version 2.6, 2017, may be used if the HCDO knows what interoperability capabilities it is seeking, what product functions support that interoperability, and which standards are to be implemented.

Current Interoperability Functionality by Specific Capability
Describe the extent to which the product conforms to the following requirements:

- *The product must have the following capabilities:*
  - *Pulse oximeter sends % oxygen saturation and pulse rate data to other clinical systems in compliance with [IEEE 11073 Data Information Model].*
  - *Pulse oximeter sends clinical and technical (equipment) alarms, and upper and lower oxygen saturation and pulse rate alarm settings to other clinical systems using standard [IEEE 11073 Data Information Model].*
  - *Pulse oximeter interfaces with clinical systems and accepts data and control to set alarm limits [and averaging time and sensitivity mode].*

Current Interoperability Functionality by Use Case
Describe the extent to which the product conforms to the following requirements:
- *The product must implement the HITSP Lab Results Reporting (EHR) Use Case, which is*
  - *HITSP Interoperability Specification 1 (IS 01) Version 3.1, recognized 2009, as described at http://www.hitsp.org/InteroperabilitySet_Details.aspx?MasterIS=true&InteroperabilityId=44&PrefixAlpha=1&APrefix=IS&PrefixNumeric=01*
  - *The HITSP Lab Results Reporting (EHR) Use Case requires partial or complete compliance and implementation of the following standards:*
    › *Health Level 7 (HL7) Versions 2.5 and 2.5.1*
    › *HL7 Clinical Document Architecture (CDA) Release 2.0*
    › *IETF RFC 2818: Hypertext Transfer Protocol (HTTP) over Transport Layer Security (TLS)*
    › *HL7 Version 3 Standard: Role Based Access Control (RBAC) Healthcare Permissions Catalog, Release 1*
    › *HL7 Version 3.0 Privacy Consent–related specifications*
    › *IETF RFC 1305: Network Time Protocol (Version 3)*
    › *IHTSDO Systematized Nomenclature of Medicine Clinical Terms (SNOMED CT)*
    › *Logical Observation Identifiers Names and Codes (LOINC)*
    › *OASIS Security Assertion Markup Language (SAML) Version 2.0*
    › *OASIS WS-Federation Version 1.1*
    › *OASIS WS-Trust Version 1.3*
    › *OASIS eXtensible Access Control Markup Language (XACML) Version 2.0*
    › *Unified Code for Units of Measure (UCUM)*

Future Interoperability Functionality by Use Case
Describe the extent to which the product conforms to the following requirements:
  [By January 1, 2019, within 12 months of contract award] the product must implement the

- *HITSP Lab Results Reporting (EHR) Use Case, which is HITSP Interoperability Specification 1 (IS 01) Version 3.1, recognized 2009, as described at* http://www.hitsp.org/InteroperabilitySet_Details.aspx?MasterIS=true& InteroperabilityId=44&PrefixAlpha=1&APrefix=IS&PrefixNumeric=01
    › *The HITSP Lab Results Reporting (EHR) Use Case requires partial or complete compliance with and implementation of the following standards:*
    › *Health Level 7 (HL7) Versions 2.5 and 2.5.1*
    › *HL7 Clinical Document Architecture (CDA) Release 2.0*
    › *IETF RFC 2818: Hypertext Transfer Protocol (HTTP) over Transport Layer Security (TLS)*
    › *HL7 Version 3 Standard: Role Based Access Control (RBAC) Healthcare Permissions Catalog, Release 1*
    › *HL7 Version 3.0 Privacy Consent related specifications*
    › *IETF RFC 1305: Network Time Protocol (Version 3)*
    › *IHTSDO Systematized Nomenclature of Medicine Clinical Terms (SNOMED CT)*
    › *Logical Observation Identifiers Names and Codes (LOINC)*
    › *OASIS Security Assertion Markup Language (SAML) Version 2.0*
    › *OASIS WS-Federation Version 1.1*
    › *OASIS WS-Trust Version 1.3*
    › *OASIS eXtensible Access Control Markup Language (XACML) Version 2.0*
    › *Unified Code for Units of Measure (UCUM)*

RFP TEXT EXAMPLE 2: DESCRIPTION OF ALL CURRENT AND PLANNED INTEROPERABILITY

Capabilities and Related Functionality

Alternatively, the health care organization may wish to request in a Request for Information (RFI) a complete description of the product's "current" interoperability capabilities, but not call for any particular function or standard. The below example provided from MD FIRE also includes language anticipating the possibility that a respondent will engage in product development to satisfy the requirements of the health care delivery organization.

Please include in the RFI response the approach and plans for interoperability of your product(s), specifically:

- *all interoperable interface standards, technology standards, terminology standards, communication standards, and design guidelines that the products will implement and comply with (including but not limited to USB, WiFi, ZigBee, Bluetooth, HL7, and Continua Design Guidelines).*

For each standard and guideline, describe:
- *the current and proposed scope of compliance with each standard and guideline, including but not limited to the exact specifications and guideline versions;*
- *a description of the current and proposed product functions that are interoperable and supported by the standards and guidelines; and*
- *an estimate of the [not to exceed, time and materials] cost and schedule to implement the proposed capabilities and standards listed above. If updates or compliance are included in the regular maintenance agreement, please describe those terms.*

The following clause would be inserted only if the health care organization intends to fund some or all of the company's product development work that is necessary to meet actual contract or RFP requirements.
- *Describe your process for demonstration, acceptance testing, and certification and validation of the product's interoperability for the standards listed above. If you propose to provide independent validation and verification of capability, the full price of that effort should be described.*
- *Describe your processes for product maintenance and upgrades to accommodate new interface technology, new interface standards, updated interface standards, or new product functionality.*

MODULAR OPEN SYSTEMS ARCHITECTURE LANGUAGE

Interoperability steering groups and procurement teams within health care organizations and networks may find the *DoD Open Systems Architecture Contract Guidebook for Program Managers,* v1.1 (DoD Open Systems Architecture Data Rights Team, 2013) useful in developing procurement strategies and contract languages. The guidebook includes the following items that procurement teams can tailor for their respective "open systems" declaration statements and general vendor guidance:

Modular Open Systems Architecture—highlights the need for contractors to describe their approach to modularization of their product and emphasizes the need for these modules to be of a size that supports competitive acquisition as well as reuse.

Technology Insertion—highlights the importance of the contractor's use of an architectural approach supportive of the rapid and affordable insertion and refreshment of technology through modular design, the use of open standards, and open interfaces.

Interface Design and Management—outlines the level of detail needed related to the description of interfaces between all components and systems, including but not limited to mechanical, electrical (power and signal wiring), software, firmware, and hardware interface specifications.

Treatment of Proprietary or Vendor-Unique Elements—emphasizes the importance of requiring the contractor to (a) explain the use of proprietary, vendor-unique, or closed components or interfaces and (b) identify and justify proprietary, vendor-unique, or closed interfaces, code modules, hardware, firmware, or software to be used. Further, the guidebook underscores the importance of requiring the contractor to demonstrate that proprietary elements do not preclude or hinder other component or module developers from interfacing with or otherwise developing, replacing, or upgrading open parts of the system.

Open Business Practices—highlights the importance of describing how modularity of the system design promotes the identification of multiple sources of supply and/or repair, and supports flexible business strategies that enhance subcontractor competition.

Use of Standards—prioritizes the order of importance of standards based on the nature of those standards (descending importance):

- standards as specified within the contract's commercial standards;
- standards developed by international or national industry standards bodies that have been widely adopted by industry;
- standards adopted by industry consensus-based standards bodies and widely adopted in the marketplace; and
- de facto standards (those widely adopted and supported in the marketplace).

Technical Supplement—Section 4

LESSONS FROM OTHER INDUSTRIES

CASE STUDY 1
SUBMARINE FORCE'S OPEN BUSINESS MODEL APPROACH

Challenges of a closed business model

By the mid-1990s, it had become apparent to the US Navy's submarine community that their "acoustic superiority"—the undersea margin of technological superiority—had significantly diminished in light of advances in Russian and Chinese submarine technology. The majority of the submarine fleet lost the ability to maintain tactical control over their adversaries, including the ability to detect and localize the adversary through underwater sound. Although an upgrade was necessary, the acquisition mechanisms at the time were too slow in delivery and too expensive to execute. With a recent end to the Cold War, funding for submarine sonar improvements was cut by more than half. How would the United States regain acoustic superiority quickly on only a fraction of the funding previously available?

The traditional change approach involved contracting with the original equipment manufacturer, (i.e., the "prime contractor"), to design, develop, and field changes to the legacy system. A system update via this traditional approach had already been underway, estimated to take 6 years to complete. Under this approach, the unique military requirements would have dictated one-of-a-kind solutions for a set of compatible hardware and software. Before this time, the system design, development, and fielding had been entirely under the purview of a prime contractor. The "prime" hired and controlled third-party subcontractors as needed.

Aligning leadership to change the status quo

Instead, the submarine community embarked on a revolutionary approach to acquiring and improving their primary tactical control tool: sonar. The objectives were to (1) improve performance faster, (2) deliver additional improvements seamlessly when required, (3) make improvements available to all classes of submarines, and (4) implement an open system based on commercial-off-the-shelf (COTS) technology.

Under the new approach (known as acoustic rapid commercial-off-the-shelf insertion, or A-RCI), the navy modified the prime contract that previously included subcontracting third parties. Instead, the third parties became under direct contract to the navy. The prime contractor's new role became that of an integrator working in a collaborative arrangement with independent hardware and software vendors. The contracts for both the prime and the third parties stipulated that the recognition of success at system certification be either for all parties or not at all. Improved sonar performance capabilities were delivered in a phased approach in one-year increments. Each phase provided significant tactical improvement.

The acquisition strategy involved (1) maximizing the use of products that were not exclusively for governmental use, (2) institutionalizing software reuse, (3) pooling disparate upgrades to the existing legacy system into a single COTS-based development program, and (4) sharing talents and resources among program offices. In short, leverage, leverage, leverage.

Demonstrating initial benefits and garnering support

Because of this revised open environment approach, the U.S. Navy prevented any single vendor from dominating the submarine sonar system development process. By opening up opportunities for other qualified vendors, the new approach reduced barriers to using commercial equipment.

To illustrate this point, phase 1 of A-RCI involved the implementation of a new commercial off-the-shelf signal processor designed to interoperate with the legacy sonar system. The software for this new processor was designed by a small business under a Small Business Innovative Research grant. It was developed and delivered to the submarine fleet in 18 months, and it showed new capability and better performance than what was expected under the legacy approach for 6 years. Moreover, it was inexpensive, given its capacity. With the success of Phase 1, the submarine fleet sponsors and Congress supported the decision to proceed with the remaining phases.

Realizing the benefits of the modular contracting model over time

By that time, this new approach allowed new methods and techniques to be implemented and tested on a 12- to 18-month cycle. An active peer review process, known as advanced processor build (APB), was created to allow rapid building and testing of sonar software prototypes for the A–RCI's computing platform. Rather than competing, scientists now collaborated in rapidly implementing techniques that would have taken years to mature in a traditional environment. For instance, the submarine sonar operators' success rates doubled with the incorporation of the first APB and quadrupled with the second.

The keys to APB success are (1) sharing information across organizations to create the full story, (2) data-driven testing (build-test-build), (3) peer review of new developments, (4) verification of technology before implementation, (5) continuing assessments and measurements, and (6) significant end-user (e.g., fleet user) involvement. Understandably, the submarine fleet end user was the strongest advocate for this new approach.

At its 8-year anniversary, A–RCI had been installed on more than 50 submarines with at least four generations of hardware and software upgrades. According to an internal study, compared with the observed costs over the 10-year previous legacy period, the cumulated 10-year post-A–RCI introduction represented a cost reduction of one-sixth for development and one-eighth for operation and support.

Lessons learned

Although health care's missions and goals may diverge from those of the U.S. Navy, the extent to which a lack of interoperability hinders the timeliness and efficiency of technology investment draws many parallels. There are several lessons learned from the success of A–RCI:

1. Own the architecture and the data, not necessarily the components, while mandating the use of common, nonproprietary interfaces.
2. Focus on not only the technical but also the business environments.
3. Involve the end user in the design process.
4. Do not "eat the elephant in one bite". Follow an incremental approach with measurable improvements at each stage.
5. Recognize and plan to counter the inertia of the incumbency that will resist changes potentially affecting their business model.
6. Make sure leaders are held accountable and being rewarded for success.
7. Ensure transparency, as it is crucial to maintaining the integrity of the process.
8. Make decisions based on data-driven analyses of alternatives, rather than politics or business relationships.
9. Develop road maps that provide comprehensive information on capabilities, resources, time frames, and options. Keep them current and make them available to the entire community.

CASE STUDY 2

ADVANCE EXPLOSIVE ORDNANCE DISPOSAL ROBOTIC SYSTEM (AEODRS)

Challenges of a closed business model

Unmanned ground vehicle (UGV) systems have replaced the need for humans in various tasks. These robots have shown significant benefit to disaster relief, first responders, the military, and law enforcement by conducting tasks that are infeasible, dangerous, or even life-threatening to humans (Hinton et al. 2011; Hinton et al. 2013).

Historically, the UGV industry primarily produced and sold these robots as single systems, designed and built in accordance with proprietary architecture and communication. The different physical and electrical interfaces among robots resulted in difficulties with integrating system components and advancing new capabilities, as well as maintenance and repair. At the time, the vendors were responding to an industry incentive structure that rewarded differentiation. Proprietary platforms, data, and physical interfaces gave one vendor a competitive advantage over another, hence making systems across vendors even less interoperable.

Unmanned Ground Vehicle System

SOURCE: Hinton et al. 2013

Aligning authority to change the status quo

The U.S. Navy's Advanced Explosive Ordnance Disposal Robotic System (AEODRS) program was established to change the U.S. Navy's existing paradigm of reliance on closed and proprietary technical solutions. The program introduced an open and modular approach for acquiring these systems (Hinton et al. 2011).

Acting as the primary consumer, the U.S. Navy attempted to engage vendors to develop the modular architecture and define the necessary set of requirements, performance specifications, and interface control documents (ICDs). Despite its laudable goal, there was significant skepticism from within the Department of Defense and significant pushback from the vendor community.

Designing a prototype to establish specifications and support

To break through this challenge, the U.S. Navy developed a prototype (hardware and software) solution to define the system's architecture, interfaces, and specifications. This AEODRS prototype served to prove to stakeholders and the industry that the promise of open and interoperable modular robotic systems was tangible. The development of the prototype forced the tough trade-offs in setting the standards of the future: too much specificity would stifle future innovation, but loose specifications would render themselves useless if interpretations varied widely. The AEODRS program took what were once single systems and divided them into subsystems with specific *capability modules* (Kozlowski et al. 2010; Hinton et al. 2013). These modules set the foundation for architecture and interfaces to enable plug-and-play interoperability.

The AEODRS prototype specified clear and concise system requirements, documented performance specifications for each module, and created interface control documents based on existing industry standards. The prototype provided the DoD with the performance specification and ICDs required to procure an individual item. In this case, the U.S. Navy (purchaser) served as the central authority, controlling the architecture, interfaces, and specifications (Hinton et al. 2017).

Realizing the benefits of an open business model

In the past, vendors competed by keeping their systems closed, meaning that only the vendor knew the underlying data and the way data were exchanged. As the industry shifted toward openness, well-defined interfaces became standard in accordance with specifications endorsed by a central authority (in this case the DoD). At the beginning, some perceived this open data structure as a threat to intellectual property. As the industry evolved, however, vendors were provided a platform for true innovation. The competition between vendors shifted from competing on proprietary data and interfaces to competing on performance capabilities.

The AEODRS prototype and the subsequent adoption of the AEODRS Common Architecture enabled the UGV industry to solve various operational challenges, reduce the time and cost to integrate, and facilitate a shift in the industry toward innovation. The well-defined interfaces and modules allow small and large manufacturers to compete through performance of novel capabilities and enable the integration of new capabilities on a more frequent basis (Hinton et al. 2011).

REFERENCES

114th Congress. 2015. 21st Century Cures Act, H.R. 34.

American Hospital Association (AHA). 2018. The regulatory burden on hospitals and health systems, February 2018. Available from: http://trustees.aha.org/newdeliverymodels/Regulatory%20Overload%202018.pdf.

Cantwell, E., and K. McDermott. 2016. Making technology talk: How interoperability can improve care, drive efficiency, and reduce waste. Healthcare Financial Management Association, May 2016. Available from: http://medicalinteroperability.org/wp-content/uploads/2016/04/Making-Technology-Talk_HFM-reprint_May2016.pdf.

CAP Today. 2011. Feature story. College of American Pathologists. Available from: http://www.captodayonline.com/Archives/0211/0211d_poc.html.

Dixon, B. E., and M. Hosseini. 2017. Consolidating CCD documents from multiple sources. HIMSS Annual Conference and Exhibition, February 19–23, 2017. Available from: http://www.himssconference.org/sites/himssconference/files/pdf/7.pdf.

DoD Open Systems Architecture Data Rights Team. 2013. *DoD open systems architecture contract guidebook for program managers,* v1.1, June 2013. Available from: http://www.acqnotes.com/Attachments/Open%20System%20Architecture%20(OSA)%20Contract%20Guidebook%20for%20Program%20Managers%20June%202013.pdf.

Duteau, J., and J. Madra. 2016. *Introduction to CDA and C-CDA.* HIMSS 2016. Available from: https://www.hl7.org/documentcenter/public_temp_1E66A99B-1C23-BA17-0C52645407C841CF/calendarofevents/himss/2016/Introduction%20to%20Clinical%20Document%20Architecture%20(CDA)%20and%20Consolidated%20CDA%20(C-CDA).pdf.

Fenves, S. J., E. Subrahmanian, P. Goyal, J. L. Angbo, F. Daoud, and R. D. Sriram. *The Architecture Development Facilitator (ADF) first year report, March 2007, NIST interagency/internal report (NISTIR)—7411.* Available from: https://www.nist.gov/publications/architecture-development-facilitator-adf-first-year-report.

Health Level Seven International. 2017. *HL7 standards—section 5: Implementation guides.* Available from: http://www.hl7.org/implement/standards/product_section.cfm?section=5.

Health Level Seven International Wiki. 2017. Devices on FHIR. Available from: http://wiki.hl7.org/index.php?title=Devices_on_FHIR#HL7_DEV_WG_FHIR_Projects_.28formal.29.

HealthIT.gov. 2017. C-CDA Scorecard, version: 3.1.5. Released June 26, 2017. Available from: https://sitenv.org/ccda-smart-scorecard/.

Hinton, M. A., J. M. Burck, K. R. Collins, M. S. Johannes, E. W. Tunste Jr., and M. J. Zeher. 2013. Integration of advanced explosive ordnance disposal robotic systems within a modular open systems architecture. *Johns Hopkins APL Technical Digest* 32(3), 595–604.

Hinton, M. A., M. J. Zeher, and G. Osier. 2017. Personal communication with JHU/APL.

Hinton, M. A., M. J. Zeher, M. V. Kozlowski, and M. S. Johannes. 2011. Advanced explosive ordnance disposal robotic system (AEODRS): A common architecture revolution. *Johns Hopkins APL Technical Digest* 30(3), 256–266.

IEEE Computer Society. 1991. *IEEE standard computer dictionary: A compilation of IEEE standard computer glossaries.* Institute of Electrical and Electronics Engineers (IEEE), IEEE 610–1990, January 18, 1991. Available from: http://ieeexplore.ieee.org/stamp/stamp.jsp?arnumber=182763.

IEEE Standards Association. 2017. *Healthcare IT standards.* Available from: https://standards.ieee.org/findstds/standard/health care_it.html.

Integrating the Healthcare Enterprise. 2016. *IHE technical frameworks.* Available from: https://www.ihe.net/Technical_Frameworks/.

Kozlowski, M. V., M. Hinton, and M. Johannes. 2010. *Toward a common architecture for the Advanced Explosive Ordnance Disposal Robotic Systems (AEODRS) family of unmanned ground vehicles.* Proc. 2010 NDIA Ground Vehicle Systems Engineering and Technology Symposium, Vehicle Electronics and Architecture (VEA) Mini-Symposium, Dearborn, MI, paper 213.

MD FIRE. 2018. *Medical device free interoperability requirements for the enterprise,* version 2.6. Available from: http://mdpnp.mgh.harvard.edu/projects/md-fire/.

Microsoft. 2017. *What is middleware?.* Microsoft Azure. Available from: https://azure.microsoft.com/en-us/overview/what-is-middleware/.

NASA. 2007. *NASA systems engineering handbook.* NASA/SP-2016-6105 Rev 2. Available from: https://ntrs.nasa.gov/archive/nasa/casi.ntrs.nasa.gov/20080008301.pdf.

National Institute of Standards and Technology (NIST). 2014. *Framework for improving critical infrastructure cybersecurity* version 1.0. Available from: https://

www.nist.gov/sites/default/files/documents/cyberframework/cybersecurity-framework-021214.pdf.

Object Management Group. 2017. *Unified modeling language.* Available from: https://www.omg.org/spec/UML.

Object Management Group. 2017. *Systems modeling language.* Available from: www.omgsysml.org.

Oemig, F., and R. Snelick. 2016. *Healthcare interoperability standards compliance handbook: Conformance and testing of healthcare data exchange standards.* Springer.

Office of the National Coordinator for Health IT. 2012. *Request for proposal (RFP) template for health information technology.* Available from: https://www.healthit.gov/resource/request-proposal-rfp-template-health-information-technology.

Office of the National Coordinator for Health IT. 2016. *EHR contracts untangled.* Available from: https://www.healthit.gov/sites/default/files/EHR_Contracts_Untangled.pdf.

Office of the National Coordinator for Health IT. 2017a. *Interoperability standards advisory,* reference edition. Available from: https://www.healthit.gov/sites/default/files/2017_isa_reference_edition-final.pdf.

Office of the National Coordinator for Health IT. 2017b. Demystifying patient matching algorithms. *Health IT Buzz*, May 1, 2017. Available from: https://www.healthit.gov/buzz-blog/interoperability/demystifying-patient-matching-algorithms/.

Office of the Assistant Secretary for Preparedness and Response, Health and Human Services. 2017. *Public health emergency.* Available from: https://www.phe.gov/Preparedness/planning/CyberTF/Pages/default.aspx.

Palfrey, J., and U. Gasser. 2012. *Interop: The promise and perils of highly interconnected systems.* New York: Basic Books.

PC Magazine. 2017. Encyclopedia. Available from: https://www.pcmag.com/encyclopedia/term/37856/api.

Personal Connected Health Alliance. 2017. Available from: http://www.pchalliance.org/.

Personal communication, P. Schluter, November 2017.

Reves, J. G. 2003. "Smart pump" technology reduces errors. *Anesthesia Patient Safety Foundation (APSF) Newsletter* 18(1). Available from: https://www.apsf.org/newsletters/html/2003/spring/smartpump.htm.

Selva, T., and S. Katz. 2017. Choosing the right IT projects to deliver strategic value. HIMSS Annual Conference and Exhibition, February 22, 2017. Available from: http://www.himssconference.org/sites/himssconference/files/pdf/206.pdf.

Sequoia Project. 2015. *A framework for cross-organizational patient identity management—draft for public review and comment.* November 10, 2015. Available from: http://sequoiaproject.org/framework-for-cross-organizational-patient-identity-matching/.

Sinsky, C., L. Colligan, L. Li, M. Prgomet, S. Reynolds, L. Goeders, J. Westbrook, M. Tutty, and G. Blike. 2016. Allocation of physician time in ambulatory practice: A time and motion study in 4 specialties. *Annals of Internal Medicine.* Available from: http://annals.org/aim/article/2546704/allocation-physician-time-ambulatory-practice-time-motion-study-4-specialties.

SMART on FHIR. 2017. *RFP language for buying SMART-compatible HIT.* Available from: https://smarthealthit.org/2014/10/rfp-language-for-buying-smart-compatible-hit/.

Taylor, S., and R. Snelick. 2016. *The role of standards in preventing and mitigating health IT patient safety risks.* Available from: https://www.nist.gov/sites/default/files/documents/2016/09/08/sheryl_taylor_and_rob_snelick_standards_for_interoperability-life_and_death_implications_in_health_it.pdf.

Appendix B

NAM STAKEHOLDER MEETING AGENDA AND PARTICIPANTS

PROCURING DIGITAL INTEROPERABILITY IN HEALTH CARE

A meeting of the Executive Leadership Network for a Continuously Learning Health System
NAM Leadership Consortium for a Value & Science-Driven Health System

Sponsored by the Gordon and Betty Moore Foundation

January 30, 2018
National Academy of Sciences Building
Lecture Room
2101 Constitution Ave. NW
Washington, DC 20418

Meeting focus: Driving health care interoperability through collaborative procurement strategies

Context: Consideration of the NAM Special Publication: "Procuring Interoperability: Achieving High-Quality, Connected, and Patient-Centered Care Through Strategic Acquisition Specifications"

Key discussion questions:

1. Core elements. What are the core elements of digital interoperability in health and health care?
2. Status and consequences. What is the status of digital interoperability in HIT, and what are the health outcomes and efficiency consequences of the shortfalls?

3. Approaches and barriers. What are the primary approaches to advancing interoperability at the organizational and system levels, and the primary barriers to success?
4. Procurement strategy. How have digital procurement strategies worked in other industries, and how can systematic and collaborative strategies by health care organizations drive transformative interoperability for the benefit of their patients?
5. CEO and CIO leadership opportunities. What intra-organizational and system-wide collaborative activities can turn HIT purchasing strategies into a transformative tool for advancing health care safety, outcomes, and value?

8:30 AM   Welcome, opening remarks, and introductions

Welcome and call to order
  Michael McGinnis, National Academy of Medicine

Opening remarks
  Victor Dzau, President, National Academy of Medicine
  Harvey Fineberg, President, Gordon and Betty Moore Foundation

Review of the flow of the day
  Claire Wang, National Academy of Medicine

Brief remarks from the US Secretary of Veterans Affairs
  David Shulkin, Department of Veterans Affairs

8:45 AM   Interoperability in health and health care: an overview

- Definitions and core elements of interoperability in health and health care
- Current status of digital interoperability in health
- Roles and status of standards
- Existing initiatives promoting interoperability
- Barriers and rate-limiting factors, including demand- and supply-side forces

Moderator: *Michael McGinnis,* National Academy of Medicine
  Presentations:
Federal interoperability road map and the 21st Century Cures Act
  Don Rucker, Office of the National Coordinator for Health IT, HHS

Features and status of interoperability in US health care
  Julia Adler-Milstein, University of California, San Francisco

Leveraging health IT for patient care: practical considerations
  Christopher Ross, Mayo Clinic

Policy and marketplace drivers for digital interoperability
  Chantal Worzala, American Hospital Association

Interoperability: progress, barriers, and key initiatives
  Micky Tripathi, Massachusetts eHealth Collaborative

Open Discussion

10:00 AM   Break

10:15 AM   Procuring interoperability: the NAM Special Publication

- Background to the project and organization of the activities
- Current profile of technology procurement in health and health care
- Opportunities and strategies identified in the project
- Technical components and starting points
- Interoperability procurement experiences from sectors outside health

Report background, organization, and action priorities
  Peter Pronovost, Johns Hopkins Medicine

Discussants:
  Sezin Palmer, Johns Hopkins University, Applied Physics Laboratory
  Meredith Karney, Center for Medical Interoperability
  Oscar Marcia, Eonti
  Bill Johnson, US Navy (former)

Open Discussion

**11:30 AM   Procuring interoperability: system-wide strategic
                  considerations**

- System-level view of comprehensive interoperability
- Technology and infrastructure requirements
- Platform development approaches: build and license versus open-source
- Partnerships, consortia, and industry support

Panel discussion, with introductory reflections by each panelist on
1. Interoperable health IT infrastructure at points of care: key clinical scenarios
2. Path toward data liquidity and plug-and-play commercial solutions
3. Technical infrastructure: common platforms, reference architectures, certification
4. Standard development and stewardship priorities

Moderator: *Michael Johns*, Emory University

Panelists:
  Julian Goldman, Partners Healthcare
  Laurie McGraw, American Medical Association
  Ed Miller, Center for Medical Interoperability
  Andy Gettinger, Office of the National Coordinator for Health IT

Open Discussion

12:45 PM   Lunch panel: Accelerating marketplace contributions to interoperability

Panel discussion, with introductory reflections by each panelist on their company and their industry's contributions to interoperability and what accelerants they recommend.

Moderator: *Wendy Nilsen*, National Science Foundation

Panelists:
  Bram Stolk, General Electric
  David McCallie, Cerner
  Rob Klootwyk, Epic
  Chuck Martel, Anthem
  Eyal Oren, Google
  Open Discussion

1:45 PM   Procuring interoperability: strategic priorities for health care system leaders

Panel discussion among health care organization leaders on the match of the action priorities—Commit, Identify, Collaborate, Specify, and Assess—with their experience, and the most important steps toward implementation.
Moderator: *Karen Guice,* Ernst and Young

Panelists:
  VADM Raquel Bono, Defense Health Agency, Department of Defense
  Jim Jirjis, HCA Healthcare
  Charles N. Kahn III, Federation of American Hospitals
  Open Discussion

2:45 PM   Break

3:00 PM   Health care CEO perspectives

- Conditions for success
- Internal leadership opportunities
- Collaborative leadership opportunities
- How the NAM might be facilitative

Moderator: *Aneesh Chopra,* CareJourney

Reflections and recommendations:
  Toby Cosgrove, Cleveland Clinic
  Steve Safyer, Montefiore Medicine
  Christopher Ross, Mayo Clinic
  Stephanie Reel, Johns Hopkins Medicine
  Rene Cabral-Daniels, Community Care Network of Virginia
  Open Discussion

4:20 PM   Immediate priority steps—facilitated discussion
Moderator: *Peter Pronovost,* Johns Hopkins Medicine
Open Discussion

4:50 PM   Summary comments, thanks, and adjournment

Peter Pronovost, Johns Hopkins Medicine
Michael McGinnis, National Academy of Medicine

MEETING PLANNING COMMITTEE

Co-Chairs

Peter Pronovost, Johns Hopkins Medicine

Michael M. E. Johns, Emory University/Chairman Emeritus, Center for Medical Interoperability

Sezin Palmer, Johns Hopkins University Applied Physics Laboratory

Participants

Meredith Karney, Center for Medical Interoperability

Raquel Bono, Defense Health Agency, US Department of Defense

Douglas B. Fridsma, American Medical Informatics Association

Andy Gettinger, ONC, US Department of Health and Human Services

John Halamka, Beth Israel Deaconess System and Harvard Medical School

William Johnson, (US Navy—retired), WMJ Associates

Jennifer Lee, US Department of Veterans Affairs (former)

Wendy Nilsen, National Science Foundation

Craig Samitt, Anthem, Inc.

Ram D. Sriram, National Institute of Standards and Technology

Staff Officer

Y. Claire Wang, National Academy of Medicine

MEETING PARTICIPANTS

Julia Adler-Milstein, PhD
Associate Professor
School of Medicine
University of California, San Francisco

Beth Berselli, MBA
Program Officer
Gordon and Betty Moore Foundation

Lauren Block, MPA
Program Director, Health
National Governors Association

Meryl Bloomrosen, MBI, MBA
Senior Director, Federal Affairs
Premier

Vice Admiral Raquel C. Bono
Director, Defense Health Agency
Medical Corps, United States Navy
Military Health Agency
US Department of Defense

Rene Cabral-Daniels, JD, MPH
Chief Executive Officer
Community Care Network of Virginia

Ed Cantwell
President and Chief Executive Officer
Center for Medical Interoperability

Lauren Choi, MA, JD
Vice President, Policy Development
and Member Relations
Network for Excellence in Health
Innovation

Aneesh Chopra, MD
President
CareJourney

Kyle Nicholls Cobb
Senior Director, Quality Measurement
National Quality Forum

Delos "Toby" M. Cosgrove, MD
Executive Advisor
Former Chief Executive Officer and
President
Cleveland Clinic

Christine Dymek, EdD
Director, Health IT Division
Agency for Healthcare Research and
Quality

Shahram Ebadollahi, PhD, MBA, MS
Vice President, Innovations
Chief Science Officer
IBM Watson Health Group

Jon Eisenberg, PhD
Director, Computer Science and
Telecommunications Board
National Academies of Sciences,
Engineering, and Medicine

Jim Fackler, MD
Associate Professor
Johns Hopkins University

Douglas B. Fridsma, MD, PhD, FACP, FACMI
President and Chief Executive Officer
American Medical Informatics Association

Andy Gettinger, MD
Chief Clinical Officer
Office of the National Coordinator of Health IT
US Department of Health and Human Services

Scott Gearhart, MSEE
Principal Staff, Health Systems Engineering
Johns Hopkins University Applied Physics Laboratory

Julian M. Goldman, MD
Medical Director, Biomedical Engineering
Partners Healthcare System
Director, Medical Device Interoperability Program (MD PnP)
Massachusetts General Hospital

Aaron Goldmuntz, MBA, MHSA
Senior Vice President, Comprehensive Interoperability
Center for Medical Interoperability

Tina Grande, MHS
Senior Vice President, Policy
Healthcare Leadership Council

Evan Grossman
Vice President, Integration Services
Athenahealth

Karen Guice, MD, MPP
Executive Director and Chief Medical Officer
Ernst and Young

Richard Gundling, FHFMA, CMA
Senior Vice President, Healthcare Financial Practices
Healthcare Financial Management Association

Marianne Hamilton Lopez, PhD, MPA
Research Director
Duke-Robert J. Margolis Center for Health Policy

Michael L. Hodgkins, MD, MPH
Chief Medical Information Officer
American Medical Association

Charles Jaffe, MD, PhD
Chief Executive Officer
Health Level 7 International (HL7)

Anil K. Jain, MD
Vice President and Chief Health Information Officer
IBM Watson Health

Jim Jirjis, MD, MBA, FACP
Vice President and Chief Health Information Officer
HCA
Vanderbilt University Medical Center

Michael M. E. Johns, MD
Professor, Schools of Public Health and Medicine
Executive Vice President, Health Affairs Emeritus
Emory University

William "Bill" M. Johnson, MEE
Principal
WMJ Associates, LLC

Charles (Chip) N. Kahn III, MPH
President and Chief Executive Officer
Federation of American Hospitals

Meredith Karney, MS, MHA, RD
Vice President, Health Economics and Value
Center for Medical Interoperability

Joe Kiani, PhD (hon)
Chairman and Chief Executive Officer
Masimo Corporation
Founder
Patient Safety Movement Foundation

Rob Klootwyk, MBA
Director, Interoperability
Epic

Janet Marchibroda, MBA
Director, Health Innovation Initiative
Bipartisan Policy Center

Oscar Marcia, MSEE
President and Chief Executive Officer
Eonti

Chuck Martel, MBA
Staff Vice President, Health Care Analytics; Data Integration and Clinical Information
Anthem, Inc.

Ross D. Martin, MD, MHA
Program Director
CRISP

David McCallie, MD
Senior Vice President, Medical Informatics
Cerner

Michael J. McCoy, MD
Chief Executive Officer
Physician Technology Services

Michael McGinnis, MD, MPP
Executive Director, Leadership Consortium for a Value & Science-Driven Health System
Leonard D. Schaeffer Executive Officer
National Academy of Medicine

Laurie McGraw
Senior Vice President, Health Solutions Group
American Medical Association

Ed Miller, MSEE
Chief Technology Officer
Center for Medical Interoperability

Jeff Nadler
Chief Information Officer
Teladoc

Wendy Nilsen, PhD
Program Director
National Science Foundation

Eyal Oren, PhD
Product Manager
Google

Sezin A. Palmer, MS
National Health Mission Area
   Executive
Johns Hopkins Applied Physics Lab

Peter Pronovost, MD, PhD, FCCM
Director, Armstrong Institute for
   Patient Safety and Quality
Johns Hopkins Medicine

Matthew Quinn, MBA
Senior Advisor, Health Information
   Technology
Health Resources and Service
   Administration
US Department of Health and Human
   Services

Alan Ravitz, PE, PhD
Chief Engineer, National Health
   Mission Area
Johns Hopkins University Applied
   Physics Laboratory

Stephanie L. Reel, MBA
Chief Information Officer
Vice Provost, Information Technology
Senior Vice President, Information
   Services
Johns Hopkins University

Matt Reid, MS
Senior Health IT Consultant
American Medical Association

Lauren Riplinger, JD
Senior Director, Federal Relations
American Health Information
   Management Association

Christopher Ross, MBA
Chief Information Office
Mayo Clinic

Don Rucker, MD, MBA
National Coordinator
Office of National Coordinator for
   Health IT
US Department of Health and Human
   Services

Steven M. Safyer, MD
President and Chief Executive Officer
Montefiore Medicine

Mari Savickis, MPA
Vice President, Federal Affairs
College of Healthcare Information
   Management Executives

Loretta Schlachta-Fairchild, PhD, RN,
   FACHE
Health IT Research Program Manager
Medical Research Material Command
Defense Health Agency
US Department of Defense

Ram D. Sriram, PhD
Chief, Software and Systems Division
National Institute of Standards and
Technology

Bram Stolk, MBA, PhD
Vice President and General Manager,
Global Research Organization
GE Healthcare

Micky Tripathi, PhD, MPP
President and Chief Executive Officer
Massachusetts eHealth Collaborative

Kara Tuohey, MPH
Assistant Group Supervisor, Health
Systems Engineering
Johns Hopkins University Applied
Physics Laboratory

Allison Viola, MBA
Director, Health IT Policy
Kaiser Permanente Information
Technology

Vindell Washington, MD, MHCM
Chief Medical Officer
Blue Cross and Blue Shield of Louisiana

Sandy Weininger, PhD
Electrical Safety Gatekeeper
US Food and Drug Administration

Chantal Worzala, PhD
Vice President, Health Information
and Policy Operations
American Hospital Association

Ashwini "Ash" M. Zenooz, MD
Chief Medical Officer, EHR
Modernization
US Department of Veterans Affairs

NAM Staff

Urooj Fatima
Senior Program Assistant
National Academy of Medicine

Gwen Hughes
Senior Program Assistant
National Academy of Medicine

Vivi Vo
Former Senior Program Assistant
National Academy of Medicine

Y. Claire Wang, MD, ScD
Senior Program Advisor
National Academy of Medicine

Danielle Whicher, PhD, MHS
Senior Program Officer
National Academy of Medicine

Appendix C

BIOGRAPHIES OF STEERING COMMITTEE MEMBERS AND STAFF

Vice Admiral Raquel Bono, MD, MBA, was commissioned in June 1979, obtained her baccalaureate degree from the University of Texas at Austin, and attended medical school at Texas Tech University. She completed a surgical internship and a general surgery residency at Naval Medical Center Portsmouth, and a Trauma and Critical Care fellowship at the Eastern Virginia Graduate School of Medicine. Her senior officer assignments include executive assistant to the 35th Navy Surgeon General and Chief, Bureau of Medicine and Surgery; commanding officer, Naval Hospital Jacksonville; chief of staff, deputy director Tricare Management Activity; deputy director, Medical Resources, Plans and Policy, chief of Naval Operations; command surgeon, US Pacific Command; director, National Capital Region Medical Directorate, Defense Health Agency and the 11th Chief, Navy Medical Corps. Vice Admiral Bono is a diplomat of the American Board of Surgery and has an Executive MBA from the Carson College of Business at Washington State University. Her personal decorations include the Defense Superior Service Medal (three), Legion of Merit Medal (four), Meritorious Service Medal (two), and the Navy and Marine Corps Commendation Medal (two).

Douglas Fridsma, MD, PhD, FACP, FACMI, is the president and chief executive officer of AMIA, a membership society representing 5,000 professional and student informaticians and their interests and activities in academe, industry, government, and nonprofit organizations. Dr. Fridsma is an expert in informatics, interoperability, standards, and health IT (including meaningful use). His understanding of the science and application of informatics and experience as practitioner and policy maker give him a depth of knowledge well suited to the critical challenge of transforming health and health care. Before joining AMIA, Dr. Fridsma was the chief science officer for the Office of the National Coordinator for Health Information Technology, responsible for the portfolio of technical resources needed to support the meaningful use program and health information technology interoperability. While at ONC, he developed the standards and interoperability framework to accelerate the development of technical specifications for interoperability, and in collaboration with the NIH and other federal agencies was instrumental in establishing the key priorities in the PCOR Trust fund. Before ONC, Dr. Fridsma held academic appointments at the University of Pittsburgh, Arizona State University, University of Arizona, and Mayo Clinic, and had a part-time clinical practice at the Mayo Clinic Scottsdale. He has served as a board member of HL7 and the Clinical Data Interchange Standards Consortium, where he was instrumental in developing standards that bridge clinical care and clinical research.

Andrew Gettinger, MD, serves as chief medical information officer and director of the Office of Clinical Quality and Safety for ONC. He is a professor of anesthesiology, adjunct professor of computer science at Dartmouth, and senior scholar at the Koop Institute, Geisel School of Medicine at Dartmouth, and was formerly the chief medical information officer for Dartmouth-Hitchcock and associate dean for clinical informatics at Geisel. Dr. Gettinger has extensive experience in the field of health information technology. He led the development of an electronic health record (EHR) system at Dartmouth and subsequently was the senior physician leader during Dartmouth's transition to a vendor-based EHR. Dr. Gettinger's clinical practice and research has been focused both on anesthesiology and critical care medicine, and on information technology as it applies generally to health care.

Julian M. Goldman, MD, is medical director of biomedical engineering for Partners HealthCare System, an anesthesiologist at the Massachusetts General Hospital, and director of the Program on Medical Device Interoperability based at the Massachusetts General Hospital Department of Anesthesia Critical Care and Pain Medicine, Partners HealthCare System, and CIMIT. Dr. Goldman founded the Medical Device "Plug-and-Play" (MD PnP) Interoperability research program in 2004 to promote innovation in patient safety and clinical care by leading the adoption of patient-centric integrated clinical environments. Dr. Goldman completed anesthesiology residency and fellowship training at the University of Colorado. His research fellowship was in biomedical informatics, focusing on simulation and applications for monitoring and real-time decision support. He left Colorado in 1998 as a tenured associate professor to work as an executive of a medical device company. Dr. Goldman joined Harvard Medical School and the Department of Anesthesia, Critical Care, and Pain Medicine at the Massachusetts

General Hospital in 2002, where he served as a principal anesthesiologist in the MGH "Operating Room of the Future." He is board certified in anesthesiology and clinical informatics. Dr. Goldman co-chaired the FCC mHealth Task Force, the HIT Policy Committee FDASIA Workgroup regulatory subgroup, and the FCC Consumer Advisory Committee work group on health care. He served on the National Science Foundation Directorate for Computer & Information Science & Engineering Advisory Committee, as a Visiting Scholar in the FDA Medical Device Fellowship Program, and as a member of the CDC Board of Scientific Counselors for the National Center for Public Health Informatics. He currently serves in leadership positions in several medical device standardization organizations, including chair of ISO Technical Committee 121, chair of the Use Case Working Group of the Continua Health Alliance, and co-chair of the AAMI Interoperability Working Group. Dr. Goldman is the recipient of the International Council on Systems Engineering 2010 Pioneer Award, American College of Clinical Engineering 2009 award for Professional Achievement in Technology, the 2009 AAMI Foundation/Institute for Technology in Healthcare Clinical Application Award, and the University of Colorado chancellor's "Bridge to the Future" award.

Michael M. E. Johns, MD, is professor of Medicine and Public Health at Emory University, where he served as chancellor from 2007 until 2012. His career at Emory began in 1996 when he was appointed executive vice president for Health Affairs, CEO of the Robert W. Woodruff Health Sciences Center, and chairman of the board of Emory Healthcare. As leader of the health sciences center and Emory Healthcare for 11 years, Dr. Johns engineered the transformation of the center into one of the nation's preeminent centers of education, research, and patient care. He previously served as dean of the Johns Hopkins School of Medicine and vice president for medicine at Johns Hopkins University from 1990 to 1996. Dr. Johns has been a significant contributor to many of the leading organizations and policy groups in health care, including the Institute of Medicine (IOM), the Association of American Medical Colleges, the Commonwealth Fund Task Force on Academic Health Centers, the Association of Academic Health Centers, and many others. He frequently lectures, publishes, and works with state and federal policy makers on topics ranging from the future of health professions education to national health system reform. Dr. Johns was elected to the Institute of Medicine in 1993 and has served on many IOM committees. He received his bachelor's degree from Wayne State University and his medical degree with distinction at the University of Michigan Medical School.

William M. Johnson, MEE, is an independent consultant and sole proprietor of WMJ Associates LLC, advising government and industry on management and leadership matters involving the acquisition of complex systems. He is a graduate of Cornell University (BSEE, MEE) and Harvard JFK School of Government (SONS). With 37 years of experience as government engineer and program manager, he is widely acclaimed as a pioneer in technical and business process transformation within the navy and the Department of Defense. His approach to implementation of "open architecture" continues to be heralded as the "poster child" model. Mr. Johnson's role in this effort is featured in the book *Collaborate or Perish! Reaching Across Boundaries in a Networked World* (2012) published by Random House. His programs have been the subject of numerous case studies by various organizations, including Harvard and the Naval Post Graduate School. Mr. Johnson is a recipient of the Navy Distinguished Civilian Award, its highest civilian honor.

Meredith Karney, MS, MHA, RD, is vice president of Health Economics and Value at the Center for Medical Interoperability. She leads the center's efforts to analyze economic and qualitative implications of data interoperability and to develop opportunities for value creation across the US health care sector. Before joining the center, Ms. Karney led health care research and project engagements for Professor Michael Porter at the Institute for Strategy and Competitiveness at the Harvard Business School. She partnered with innovative providers and payers to design value-based health care delivery and reimbursement models, and developed processes to enable improved operational and clinical health care outcomes in coordination with the International Consortium for Health Outcomes Measurement. Previously, Ms. Karney led cost measurement pilot projects at the Medical University of South Carolina that used time-driven, activity-based cost accounting frameworks and designed and negotiated bundled pricing models. She is a registered dietitian and worked and trained in clinical nutrition at Emory Healthcare. Ms. Karney holds a master of health administration and management degree from the Medical University of South Carolina and a master of science degree from Georgia State University.

Sezin A. Palmer, MS, is the first Mission Area Executive for National Health at the Johns Hopkins University Applied Physics Laboratory, which was recognized by Fast Company in 2016 as one of the most innovative companies in health care. In this role, she is responsible for technical and programmatic leadership of the laboratory's work in health. Before her current appointment, Ms. Palmer served as the Mission Area Executive for Research and Exploratory

Development. Under her leadership, APL made significant contributions to the fields of neuroscience, biomechanics, intelligent systems, and material science. Previously, Ms. Palmer held leadership positions in the laboratory's Undersea Warfare mission area, where she was responsible for the technical and programmatic oversight of numerous Navy programs in submarine warfare, anti-submarine warfare and mine-countermeasures capability development. She also served as the laboratory's representative to the commander, Pacific Fleet staff. Additionally, from 2002 to 2005, Ms. Palmer served as a panel member of the chief of Naval Operations Mine Countermeasures Technical Advisory Group and from 2010 to 2012 as a member of the Chief of Naval Operations Submarine Security Working Group. Before joining the laboratory in 2000, Ms. Palmer held technical positions at the US Naval Research Laboratory and served as an analyst in the Central Intelligence Agency's Directorate of Intelligence. Ms. Palmer earned a bachelor of science degree in electrical engineering from the University of Maryland and a master of science degree in electrical engineering from Johns Hopkins University.

Peter Pronovost, MD, PhD, FCCM, is a patient safety champion; a practicing critical care physician; a member of the National Academy of Medicine; a prolific researcher, publishing more than 800 peer-reviewed publications; and a global thought leader, informing US and global health policy. His scientific work leveraging checklists to reduce catheter-related bloodstream infections has saved thousands of lives and earned him high-profile accolades, including being named one of the 100 most influential people in the world by *Time* magazine and receiving a coveted MacArthur Foundation "genius grant" in 2008. The life-saving intervention has been implemented state by state across the United States. Today, these catheter infections that used to kill as many people as breast or prostate cancer have been reduced by 80 percent. After demonstrating the ability to eliminate one harm in most health systems, Dr. Pronovost is seeking to eliminate all harms.

Craig Samitt, MD, serves as executive vice president and chief clinical officer for Anthem. As a member of the company's executive leadership team, he is responsible for establishing, leading, and executing Anthem's overall clinical vision and strategy with a focus on improving patient outcomes and delivering value-based care to Anthem's nearly 40 million medical members. Dr. Samitt oversees Anthem's clinical operations, including health care analytics, corporate medical and pharmacy policy, health care management and quality, program integrity, and community health initiatives. He is also responsible for the Provider

Solutions team, which is transforming the provider experience by supporting and delivering a seamless business interaction across Anthem's industry-leading portfolio of provider partnerships and payment innovation models. Additionally, Dr. Samitt has responsibility for HealthCore, Anthem's clinical outcomes research subsidiary, and AIM Specialty Health, Anthem's specialty benefits management subsidiary focused on promoting evidence-based care in high-risk, high-cost areas such as imaging, oncology, and specialty pharmaceuticals. Dr. Samitt is a nationally recognized health care policy expert and thought leader with more than 20 years of experience leading health care delivery and service organizations. Before joining Anthem in September 2015, Dr. Samitt served as partner and global provider practice leader of Oliver Wyman's Health & Life Sciences division, and, before that, as president and chief executive officer for HealthCare Partners, a subsidiary of DaVita HealthCare, one of the largest physician-centric delivery systems in the country. Much of Dr. Samitt's leadership career was spent as president and CEO of Dean Health System, one of the largest integrated health systems in the Midwest. Dr. Samitt serves on the board of directors of the National Committee for Quality Assurance and is serving a second three-year term as a commissioner for MedPAC, an influential, independent legislative branch agency established and appointed by the US Government Accountability Office to advise Congress on policies governing health plans and health care providers serving America's Medicare beneficiaries. Dr. Samitt previously served on the boards of Advocate Physicians Partners, Tandigm Health, the Wisconsin Statewide Health Information Network, the Wharton Healthcare Alumni Association, and the Patient-Centered Primary Care Collaborative Center for Accountable Care. He lectures extensively about the transformation of US health care, has been recognized by *Modern Healthcare* as one of the "50 Most Influential Physician Executives and Leaders," and serves as an annual faculty lecturer at the Wharton School of Business. Dr. Samitt earned his undergraduate degree from Tufts University, medical degree from Columbia University, and MBA in health care management from the Wharton School of Business. He completed medical residency in internal medicine at Boston's Brigham and Women's Hospital.

Ram D. Sriram, PhD, is the chief of the Software and Systems Division, Information Technology Laboratory, at the National Institute of Standards and Technology. He is also the lead for the NIST's Health IT Program. Before joining the Software and Systems Division, Dr. Sriram was the leader of the Design and Process group in the Manufacturing Systems Integration Division, Manufacturing Engineering Laboratory, where he conducted research on standards for interoperability of computer-aided design systems. Before joining NIST, he was on the engineering faculty (1986–1994) at the Massachusetts Institute of Technology and was instrumental in setting up the Intelligent Engineering Systems Laboratory. Dr. Sriram has co-authored or authored more than 250 publications, including several books. He was a founding co-editor of the *International Journal for AI in Engineering*. Dr. Sriram has received several awards, including an NSF's Presidential Young Investigator Award (1989); ASME Design Automation Award (2011); ASME CIE Distinguished Service Award (2014); the Washington Academy of Sciences' Distinguished Career in Engineering Sciences Award (2015); and ASME CIE division's Lifetime Achievement Award (2016). Dr. Sriram is a fellow of the American Society of Mechanical Engineers, the American Association for the Advancement of Science, the Institute of Electrical and Electronics Engineers, and the Washington Academy of Sciences, and a life member of the Association for Computing Machinery and Association for the Advancement of Artificial Intelligence. He has a B.Tech. from IIT, Madras, India, and an MS and a PhD from Carnegie Mellon University in Pittsburgh.

Ashwini M. Zenooz, MD, is the chief medical officer for the Electronic Health Record Modernization (EHRM) in the Office of Secretary at the Department of Veterans Affairs (VA). She most recently served as the deputy to the deputy undersecretary for Health Policy and Services, where she provided guidance and leadership on matters related to health care policy, strategic objectives, and policy requirements for legislatively mandated health care delivery programs. Before that, she was a Brookings Congressional Health Policy fellow in the US Senate. Dr. Zenooz is a practicing abdominal radiologist. She has held various clinical roles in the VA, including chief of imaging services at the NY Harbor Healthcare System. Her private sector radiology experience includes her practice at Brigham and Women's Healthcare System and at the Massachusetts Eye and Ear Infirmary.

NAM Staff

Y. Claire Wang, MD, ScD, is senior program advisor at the National Academy of Medicine (NAM) and associate professor of health policy and management at Columbia Mailman School of Public Health. She was trained as a physician epidemiologist and decision scientist, with expertise in health policy, outcomes research, and population health. She leads the NAM's Vital Signs initiative, which aims to catalyze the refinement and adoption of a streamlined set of parsimonious measures to provide consistent benchmark for health progress and improve system performance in the highest priority areas. As a member of the Columbia faculty, she co-directs the Obesity Prevention Initiative, a cross-disciplinary team focusing on environmental and policy approaches to preventing obesity at the community level, as well as the MPH certificate in Comparative Effectiveness and Outcomes Research. In 2015–2016, she was selected as Robert Wood Johnson Foundation health policy fellow, serving in the US Department of Health and Human Services, Office of the Assistant Secretary for Health. She obtained her medical degree from National Taiwan University and her doctorate from Harvard School of Public Health.

Marianne Hamilton Lopez, PhD, MPA, is research director of the Value-Based Payment Reform portfolio at the Margolis Center for Health Policy at Duke University. In this role, she manages the center's activities aimed at identifying barriers and facilitating implementation of new value-based payment models for pharmaceuticals, including gene therapies, and medical devices. She oversees the Developing a Path to Value-Based Reimbursement for Medical Products Consortium and partners with Duke University faculty, scholars, and external health experts to advance this work. Before joining Duke-Margolis, Dr. Hamilton Lopez was a senior program officer with the National Academy of Medicine's Leadership Consortium for a Value & Science-Driven Health System and provided strategic direction and oversight of the consortium's science and technology portfolio and the Clinical Effectiveness Research Innovation and Digital Learning Collaboratives. She was a senior manager at AcademyHealth; a public health community advisor for the United States Cochrane Center; and the Federal Women's Program manager and American Indian/Alaska Native Employment Program manager for the National Institutes of Health.

J. Michael McGinnis, MD, MPP, a physician and epidemiologist, serves at the National Academy of Medicine as senior scholar, Leonard D. Schaeffer executive officer, executive director of the Leadership Consortium for a Value & Science-Driven Health System, and the NAM Learning Health System Initiative. He is also an elected member of the NAM (1999). Previously, Dr. McGinnis was senior vice president and head of the Health Group at the Robert Wood Johnson Foundation (1999–2005). Before that, he served as assistant surgeon general and deputy assistant secretary for health at the US Department of Health and Human Services, with continuous leadership responsibility from 1977 to 1995 for federal activities in disease prevention and health promotion, a tenure unusual for political and policy posts. Chair and founder of various national efforts, key programs developed and launched at his initiative include the Healthy People national goals and objectives, the Dietary Guidelines for Americans, and the US Preventive Services Task Force, each still ongoing. Internationally, he worked in India as state director for the WHO smallpox eradication program (1974–1975), and in Bosnia as chair of the World Bank/European Commission Task Force for reconstruction in health and human services (1995–1996). Dr. McGinnis's scientific interests focus on population health and the determinants of health, his publications include approximately 200 articles and more than 20 edited books, and among his national recognitions are the public health Distinguished Service Medal (1989), Health Leader of the Year Award (1996), and Public Health Hero Award (2013). His degrees are from Berkeley (1966), UCLA (1971), and Harvard (1977); he was commencement speaker at each.

Appendix D

GLOSSARY

TERM	DEFINITION
Application Programming Interface (API)	A set of clearly defined specifications that detail how software components should interact. In health care, APIs established a standardized approach to sharing data between connected devices and systems.
Argonaut Project	A private-sector initiative to advance industry adoption of modern, open interoperability standards. The purpose of the Argonaut Project is to accelerate time to market by developing a first-generation FHIR-based API and Core Data Services specification to enable expanded information sharing for EHRs and other health IT.
Clinical Document Architecture (CDA)	A framework for clinical documents to be structured in a way through which they can be read by both humans and computers (Oemig and Snelick, 2016).
Consolidated-Clinical Document Architecture (C-CDA)	"The HL7 Consolidated CDA is an Implementation Guide which specifies a library of templates and prescribes their use for a set of specific document types" (Duteau and Madra, 2016).
Core Data Services (CDS)	Fundamental, standards-based data services that implementations of the public API are expected to provide. The CDS read/write access to both clinical documents (e.g., discharge summary) and discrete clinical data elements (e.g., allergies).
Digital Imaging and Communications in Medicine (DICOM)	An "international standard to transmit, store, retrieve, print, process, and display imaging information" (DICOM, 2018).
Health Information Exchange (HIE)	HIE allows clinicians and patients to appropriately access and securely share a patient's medical information electronically to inform timely clinical decisions. There are currently three key forms of HIE: direct exchange, query-based exchange, and consumer-mediated exchange (ONC, 2018).
Health Information Technology for Economics and Clinical Health Act (HITECH)	Enacted as part of the American Recovery and Reinvestment Act of 2009, HITECH aims to promote the adoption and meaningful use of health IT. A section of the HITECH Act also addresses the privacy and security concerns associated with the electronic transmission of health information, in part through several provisions that strengthen the civil and criminal enforcement of the HIPAA rules.
Health Level Seven International (HL7)	Founded in 1987, HL7 is a not-for-profit, standards-developing organization dedicated to "providing comprehensive framework and related standards for the exchange, integration, sharing, and retrieval of electronic health information that supports clinical practice and the management, delivery, and evaluation of health services" (HL7, 2018).

TERM	DEFINITION
Integration Profiles/ Implementation Guides	Guidelines that prescribe to developers how to apply data exchange standards for specific types of needs (i.e., use cases) to result in more common (open) interface implementations.
Interface Control Documents (ICDs)	"Details the physical interface between two system elements, including the number and types of connectors, electrical parameters, mechanical properties, and environmental constraints" (NASA, 2007).
Integrating the Healthcare Enterprise (IHE)	An initiative started in 1997 by health care industry professionals with the initial goal of improving the integration of imaging data into hospital IT infrastructure. Since then, IHE has expanded its scope to include multiple functional domains (e.g., laboratory, cardiology, and pathology) that create specific integration profile documents and provide guidance on the coordinated use of established standards such as DICOM and HL7 (Rhoads, Cooper et al., 2009).
Interoperability	"the ability of two or more systems or components to exchange information and to use the information that has been exchanged" (IEEE Computer Society, 1991).
JASON (advisory group)	JASON is an independent group of elite scientists which advises the United States government on matters of science and technology.
JavaScript Object Notation (JSON)	An open-standard file format that uses human-readable text to transmit data objects consisting of attribute-value pairs and array data types.
Macro-Tier	A tier within the health care interoperability ecosystem that represents inter-facility information exchange.
Meaningful Use/ Medicare EHR Incentive Program	An effort initiated under the HITECH Act of 2009, led by CMS and ONC, to incentivize the adoption and "meaningful use" of certified EHR technology.
Meso-Tier	A tier within the health care interoperability ecosystem that represents intra-facility information exchange.
Micro-Tier	A tier within the health care interoperability ecosystem that represents information exchange between individual actors at the point of care.
Middleware	"Middleware is software that lies between an operating system and the applications running on it. Essentially functioning as hidden translation layer, middleware enables communication and data management for distributed applications" (Microsoft, 2017).
National Evaluation System for health Technology (NEST)	Created by the FDA to "efficiently generate better evidence for medical device evaluation and regulatory decision-making" by "strategically and systematically leveraging real-world evidence and applying advanced analytics to data tailored to the unique data needs and innovation cycles of medical devices" (FDA, 2018).
N-Squared Diagram	A systems engineering tool used to identify interactions between multiple systems.
Open Architecture (OA)	A system designed so that one subsystem can be replaced with another subsystem with minimal effect on the performance of the overall system. This means both subsystems have to meet detailed specifications.
Open Business Model	A business model structured to enable organizations to compete based on the performance of their individual products (or subsystems) rather than on how information is exchanged between subsystems.
ONC Interoperability Standards Advisory	First established in 2015 and updated annually, the ONC interoperability standards advisory provides guidance on "best-of-breed" data exchange standards, integration profiles, and implementation guides based on intended purpose (i.e., use cases), maturity, and degree of adoption.

TERM	DEFINITION
Organizational Interoperability	"Standardized process (workflow) elements using business process modeling tools" (Taylor and Snelick, 2016).
Personal Connected Health Alliance	A nonprofit organization formed by the Health Information and Management Systems Society (HIMSS) that aims to mobilize a coalition of stakeholders in technology and life sciences around personal connected health. The alliance publishes and promotes adoption of the Continua Design Guidelines, an international standard for the exchange of data to and from personal health devices.
Representational state transfer (REST) and RESTful	RESTful is an API that uses HTTP requests to get, put, post, and delete data. A RESTful API is based on representational state transfer (REST) technology, an architectural style and approach to communications often used in web services development.
Semantic Interoperability	"Standardized terms/vocabulary for data interpretation,(e.g., LOINC, ICD-10CM)" (Taylor and Snelick, 2016).
Syntactic Interoperability	"Standardized data exchange formats, (e.g., HL7, XML)" (Taylor and Snelick, 2016).
Technical Interoperability	"Signals using standard protocols for technically secure data transfer, (e.g., TCP/IP)" (Taylor and Snelick, 2016).
Trusted Exchange Framework	The Trusted Exchange Framework, released by ONC in draft form in January 2018, outlines a common set of principles for trusted exchange minimum terms and conditions for trusted exchange. It is designed to bridge the gap between providers' and patients' information systems and enable interoperability across disparate health information networks (ONC, 2018) .

INITIALISMS AND ABBREVIATIONS

ACM	Alert Communication Management
ADF	Architecture Development Facilitator
ADT	Admission/Discharge/Transfer
AEODRS	Advanced Explosive Ordnance Disposal Robotic System
AHA	American Hospital Association
APB	Advanced Processor Build
API	Application Programming Interface
A-RCI	Acoustic Rapid Commercial-off-the-shelf Insertion
BCMA	Bedside Computer-assisted Medication Administration
CCD	Continuity of Care Document
C-CDA	Consolidated-Clinical Document Architecture
CDA	Clinical Document Architecture
CHPL	Certified Health IT Product List
CDS	Core Data Services
CMI	Center for Medical Interoperability
CMS	Centers for Medicare and Medicaid Services
COTS	Commercial Off-The-Shelf
CT	Consistent Time
DEC	Device Enterprise Communications
DHA	Defense Health Agency
DICOM	Digital Imaging and Communication in Medicine
DIM	Domain Information Model
DOC	Device Observation Consumer

DoD	US Department of Defense
DOR	Device Observation Reporter
DSTU	Draft Standard for Trial Use
ED	Emergency Department
EHR	Electronic Health Record
EMR	Electronic Medical Record
ERP	Enterprise Resource Planning
ERS	Endoscopy Report Software
FDA	US Food and Drug Administration
FHIR	HL7 Fast Healthcare Interoperability Resources
GPO	Group Purchasing Organizations
HCA	Hospital Corporations of America
HCDO	Health Care Delivery Organization
HIE	Health Information Exchanges
HIMSS	Health Information Management Systems Society
HIT	Health Information Technology
HITECH	Health Information Technology for Economics and Clinical Health Act
HL7	Health Level Seven
ICDs	Interface Control Documents
ICD-10 CM	International Classification of Diseases, Tenth Revision, Clinical Modification
ICU	Intensive Care Unit
IEEE	Institute of Electrical and Electronic Engineers
IEEE 11073	IEEE 11073 Healthcare Informatics Standards
IHE	Integrating the Healthcare Enterprise
ISA	Office of the National Coordinator for Health IT's Interoperability Standards Advisory
IT	Information Technology
JSON	JavaScript Object Notation

LIS	Laboratory Information System
LOINC	Logical Observation Identifiers Names and Codes
LTW	Laboratory Testing Workflow
MDIC	Medical Device Innovation Consortium
MD FIRE	Medical Device Free Interoperability Requirements for the Enterprise
MD PnP	Medical Device Plug-and-Play
MGH	Massachusetts General Hospital
MHS	Military Health System
MOSA	Modular Open System Architecture
MTF	Military Treatment Facilities
NEST	National Evaluation System for health Technology
NAM	National Academy of Medicine
NIH	National Institutes of Health
NIST	National Institute of Standards and Technology
OA	Open Architecture
ONC	Office of the National Coordinator for Health IT
OpenICE	Open-source Integrated Clinical Environment
PC	Personal Computer
PCA	Patient Controlled Analgesia
PCAST	President's Council of Advisors on Science and Technology
PCD	Patient Care Device
PDMP	Prescription Drug Monitoring Program
PIV	Point-of-Care Infusion Verification
PoC	Point of Care
REST	Representational State Transfer
RFI	Request for Information
RFP	Requests for Proposal
SMART	Substitutable Medical Applications and Reusable Technologies

SNOMED-CT   Systemized Nomenclature of Medicine—Clinical Terms

TCP/IP   Transmission Control Protocol/Internet Protocol

UGV   Unmanned Ground Vehicle

VA   Veterans Affairs

XML   eXtensible Markup Language

CPSIA information can be obtained
at www.ICGtesting.com
Printed in the USA
BVHW091645080119
537259BV00006B/10/P